SLOWING DOWN TO THE SPEED OF JOY

MATTHEW KELLY

BLUE sparrow

Copyright © 2024 Kakadu, LLC
Published by Blue Sparrow
An Imprint of Viident

To learn more about the author, visit:
www.MatthewKelly.com

ISBN: 978-1-63582-564-0 (softcover)
ISBN: 978-1-63582-565-7 (eBook)
Audiobook available from Audible

International and foreign rights are available for this title.
For information, please email info@Viident.com
www.Viident.com

Design by Todd Detering and Maggie Barnett
Author Photo by Peggy McHale Jospeh

10   9   8   7   6   5   4   3   2   1

FIRST EDITION

Printed in the United States of America

TABLE OF CONTENTS

PART FOUR: THE SECRET OF LIFE

THE JAR OF LIFE

You may have heard this story. It's been woven into the fabric of our culture. But the untold truth of the story is what we need today. See if you can spot it.

Once upon a time there was a university professor who wanted to teach his students the importance of prioritizing how we spend our time.

The professor stood in front of his class with a large glass jar and several rocks on the table before him. Taking the empty jar, he began to fill it with the rocks. When all the rocks had been placed in the jar they reached the brim.

"Is the jar full?" he asked his students and the class agreed that it was.

Reaching under the table, the professor brought out a small bucket of pebbles. Pouring them into the jar, he shook it gently, allowing the pebbles to make their way into the space around the rocks.

"Is the jar full?" he asked again.

It looked full, but his class was reluctant to agree this time.

Next, the professor took a box of sand and added it to the jar. Shaking it gently again, he allowed the sand to settle into the crevices between the rocks and the pebbles.

"Is the jar full now?" he asked.

The students were still a little dubious but agreed that it was. All except one student.

"Why?" the professor asked her.

Standing up, she walked down toward the front of the lecture hall. In her hand she held a bottle of water. Taking the cap off, she poured the water into the jar and the water was quickly absorbed by the sand. The other students laughed and cheered.

Everyone now agreed that the jar was indeed full.

The professor then reached beneath the table, retrieved another large glass jar, another bucket of pebbles, another box of sand, and placed them on the table before the class.

"May I have a volunteer?" the professor asked. A young man raised his hand, was called upon, and made his way to the front of the room.

This time the professor emptied the box of sand into the jar first.

"Now, see if you can fit all the rocks and pebbles into the jar," he challenged his volunteer.

The young man placed half of the rocks on top of the sand and the jar was already overflowing. He tried to dig into the sand with his hands, but that only made room for one more rock. He stood there thinking for almost five minutes. He stared at the jar and the rocks still on the table while his classmates shouted out suggestions.

"Impossible!" the student finally exclaimed in frustration.

He was right of course.

"The jar is your life," the professor went on to explain. "The rocks represent what matters most. The big stuff. If there were no pebbles and no sand, the jar would still be full, and your life would have plenty of meaning and purpose. The pebbles represent the other things that matter to you but are not essential. The sand represents the things that are urgent but not important."

The moral of the story is that if you begin with the things that are urgent but not important you won't have time for what matters most. It was a lesson about time-management and priorities.

It's a great story, but it's incomplete. It teaches a powerful lesson but opens us up to a vast error. I first heard the story as a teenager and the error contained in the story took deep root in my life.

This is the error: If you were better at managing your time, better at prioritizing your daily activity, you would be able to fit everything in.

It's not true. It doesn't matter how hard you try. You will fail. You are never going to fit everything into the jar of life.

The professor had set up the experiment to guarantee his desired outcome. There was just the right amount of rocks, pebbles, and sand to ensure they would all fit in the jar. My life isn't like that, and neither is yours.

It was rigged. It was fixed. The dice were loaded.

The professor assumes there are enough hours in the day for you to take care of all the things that matter most, all the things that matter but are not essential, and all the things that are urgent but not important. There isn't.

There weren't any rocks, pebbles, or sand left over in the professor's neatly guarded experiment. That's not true in your life or mine. Every night when we go to bed there are rocks, pebbles, and sand left on the table beside the jar.

It doesn't matter how good you are at prioritizing, there are simply too many rocks and pebbles, and too much sand, to fit in the jar. It doesn't matter how efficient you become. Everything is never going to fit. And it's not like it is even close. There is a lot that won't fit in the jar of life. The overwhelming majority of opportunities and possibilities will not fit in the jar.

The story plays right into our common delusion: We have forgotten our finitude. Finitude is the state of having limits, bounds, or an end. We are human beings, we have limits, and it is past time we started living with that in mind.

Every day we participate in an epic clash between the infinite and the finite. Your time is finite, but the possibilities are endless.

Life isn't about getting everything done. That's impossible. Our refusal to face this immutable truth has resulted in epidemic levels of dissatisfaction. This dissatisfaction has led us to doubt, question, and dislike ourselves for not being able to do something that was impossible to begin with.

We have been obsessed with efficiency since the dawn of the Industrial Revolution, and for the past 250 years we have been increasing the speed of our lives. We have more stuff, we can get more done in a day, and we have unimaginable convenience—and yet, we are stressed, anxious, overwhelmed, and dissatisfied. We have gained so much, but what have we lost? What has been the real cost?

We have lost our joy. Look around. People are manic and panicked, living lives that are harried and frenzied, with hearts that are anxious and overwhelmed. Why? To what end?

The whole world is searching for its lost joy. We've just been going about it the wrong way. The speed at which you do anything can change the whole meaning of that experience. The speed at which you do something can also completely change how you experience that experience.

A conversation that is rushed tends to feel shallow and transactional. It doesn't create a meaningful connection between two people. Speed reading diminishes comprehension and satisfaction. A rushed workout can result in injury. Rushing an important decision leads us to overlook important details. This can result in a poor decision and regret. A rushed home improvement project often ends in disaster. Eating quickly leads to indigestion and prevents us from savoring our food.

We are trying to do too much too quickly.

Speed kills enjoyment. The speed at which you do anything affects the meaning of that experience, the outcome of that activity, and the experience itself.

This is true for individual activities, but it is also true of life itself. Life isn't just about what we do. The speed at which we do things matters.

Joy erupts within us when we allow an experience to touch the very depths of our souls. That cannot be rushed.

It's time to slow down to the speed of joy.

## PART ONE

BEYOND THE JOYLESS URGENCY

THE THING I WOULD CHANGE

There are people who say they have no regrets. I'm not one of them. If I could go back and live my life all over again there are things I would change. One thing I would change is the speed at which I have lived my life. I would slow my life down, and not just a little.

For most of my life I've had a very bad reputation. Since I was thirteen years old, I have been the busiest person I knew. This isn't hyperbole. I started two businesses in high school, worked part-time jobs, played several sports competitively, and took my studies seriously. Who is the busiest person you know? I suspect the people who have known me over the past thirty years would unanimously name me. For most of my life I was proud of that, but I now realize it's a bad reputation.

The glorification of busy led me to take pride in this for a long time, but those days are long gone now. Busy isn't even the right word for it. The speed at which I was living my life seems like a form of insanity in hindsight. I was living my life like a Ferrari with no brakes.

I spent thirty years rushing from one thing to the next. Leaving one thing early, arriving at the next thing late, squeezing as much as was inhumanely possible into each day—always striving for more, better, and faster. Ambition is a brutal dictator. It's disorienting. It distorts everything. Even ambition for good things can blind us to what really matters.

Ten years ago, a friend asked me a question that was so rudimentary, and yet, I had never even considered it: "Do you feel like you are doing enough?"

The question itself was bewildering. I didn't even know how to consider the question at first. The concept of doing enough was so foreign. But the question burrowed deep in my heart and began to go to work. And at times when my schedule reached obvious levels of insanity, the question would announce itself once again: "Do you feel like you are doing enough?"

The birth of my children and the joys of family life slowed my roll a little. Spending time with my children changed my whole perspective on time. But it took another ten years before I took a sufficiently bold leap to yield meaningful fruit.

For twenty-five years I had been traveling, from one city to the next, giving thousands of presentations. This had been my life. Then five years ago, by some grace I realized that I needed to slow down. It was so counter to everything I had done in my life that I still cannot believe I did it. But I committed to take one year off from traveling and speaking.

The effects were significant and immediate. I had no idea the negative impact life on the road had been having on every aspect of my life for all those years. I had long suspected some of these costs, but I had vastly underestimated them.

Even though I wasn't traveling and had seen the positive effects of that change, I remained busy, perhaps as busy as ever. I was still busier than anyone I knew. But being in the same place every day made it harder than ever to ignore the deeper questions that were needling away at my heart.

It's easy to fall into the trap of caring too much about things that don't matter enough. Those things can be material possessions, but they can also be projects, other people's opinion, social engagements, and a myriad of things we say yes to without considering the implications.

I knew I needed to slow down, but I didn't know how. It was a life skill I had never acquired. I knew the only way to slow down was to do less, and in order to do less I had to discern what mattered most.

A few days later, I wrote in a journal, "You need to change the pace of your life. It's a choice and it is yours to make."

I'd like to be able to say I have never looked back. I'd like to be able to say it has been an unmitigated success. But I can't. The truth is: I have never failed so successfully at anything in my life. I am literally horrible at this, but the fruits of my modest successes have been amazing.

For five years I have been awkwardly attempting to live my life at the speed of joy. I'm sure my fumbling and stumbling looks like a giant trying to ride a tricycle. But the fruits are undeniable and the lessons monumental. I have learned, for example, that it is possible to accomplish great things while being peaceful and content.

When I am in the classroom of silence I wonder where the intense drive came from at such a young age. I'm sure there were all sorts of hopes and dreams, insecurities and complexes, behind that drive.

Looking back today I see a young man possessed. At times possessed by mission, at times possessed by ambition, and at times possessed by a desire to please people. I look back and know I don't want to go back.

These five years have been glorious and frustrating. Slowing down to the speed of joy has been one of the most fulfilling experiences of my life. I am by no means the patron saint of the speed of joy, but I'm a true believer in its ability to transform how we experience life.

Urgent, busy, and hurry are tyrants. I have learned many things trying to break free from them. I will share those insights with you in the pages that follow. But to be clear, the ideas on these pages are ideas I am striving to embrace, not wisdom I have made my own, yet. I struggle to implement the ideas in this book every day. Some days I do great. I delight in the speed of joy on those days and promise myself I will never go back. Other days I get seduced all over again by urgent, busy, and hurry.

Slowing down to the speed of joy is simple but difficult. I want to be clear on that from the start. You need to really want it. Otherwise, the gravitational pull of the culture will tear you away from your joy, and you will find yourself trapped in the tyranny of the urgent again. It's okay to have days like that. You will. It's inevitable and unavoidable but learn to recognize them for what they are right away. Because too many days in a row like that and you will find yourself dragged back to a place you never wanted to be ever again.

You don't have to decide right now if you want to live your life at the speed of joy. Let me make a case for the speed of joy. Let me show you the what, and the why, and the how. Let me share with you how the speed of joy will improve your health, relationships, career, personal finances, spirituality and other aspects of life. Let me reintroduce you to your raw ability to enjoy life—and then you can decide.

I will say this. The speed of joy is a thing of beauty and I suspect you will become more attracted to it with every passing page.

If you sense that attraction rising in your soul—encourage it, reflect on it, be grateful for it, and together let's find ways to make the speed of joy possible for you. I say possible, because at every turn there will be other voices telling you it's impossible. Those voices are wrong. Tell them so. Shout them down if you have to.

It is possible to slow down to the speed of joy. The frantic pace of life the culture encourages is ugly and once you experience life at the speed of joy you'll never want to go back.

In a world obsessed with doing more and doing it faster than ever, slowing down and doing less is the only sane response.

If I could go back and live my life all over again, there is one thing I would change. I'd change the speed at which I have lived my life. I can't go back, but I do intend to live my life at the speed of joy from here on out.

It is time to move beyond the joyless urgency of our times.

BREAKFAST WITH A FRIEND

This is how I discovered the speed of joy.

It all started with a breakfast meeting. Not being a morning person, I don't love breakfast meetings. But a friend was in town for less than twenty-four hours and it was our only chance to connect. So, I drove over to *Paris In Town*, a quaint little bakery and café.

Even though I was fifteen minutes early, he was already there, waiting eagerly with coffee in hand. The word I would use to describe his presence is chipper—cheerful and lively—something I have never been accused of in the morning hours. I don't drink coffee, but there are times I wish I did. This was one of them.

We did the "Hi! How are you?" thing, ordered some breakfast, and then I asked, "Fill me in, catch me up, what's happening in your life?"

As soon as my friend started speaking, red flags started flying around in my head, but I made a conscious decision to just listen. He was taking lots of wrong turns and making too many regrettable decisions and avoidable mistakes. The reason I knew all this was because they were wrong turns, regrettable decisions, and avoidable mistakes I had made myself.

But he was too close to it to see it. He was moving so fast everything was a blur. He was too busy. Insanely busy. And busy is a problem. Busy is a destroyer of joy. Busy distracts us from what matters most. It deceives us into thinking activity and productivity are the same thing. Just because you are busy doing a lot (activity) doesn't mean anything of value is being accomplished (outcome). Busy doesn't care about outcomes. Busy fixates on the urgent.

After twenty-five minutes, he came up for air, took a sip of coffee, and I asked, "Why are you so busy?"

The moment the words came out of my mouth they turned on me. My friend started answering with familiar excuses and justifications. The same excuses and justifications I had told myself hundreds of times. But I was having trouble focusing. The question kept echoing in my mind: Why are you so busy? Why are you so busy? Why are you so busy?

That single question changed my life. I made radical changes to my life. Changes I didn't believe were possible. That question led me to discover the speed of joy.

Why are you so busy? I find myself returning to this question regularly. Now I offer you the same question for your own personal reflection: Why are you so busy?

It's a question that deserves serious consideration. We all have our reasons, but they are insufficient to keep you from the speed of joy permanently. We may have good reasons. They may justify our busyness in the short term, but in the long run we can all live at the speed of joy.

A lot of our justifications for the speed and busyness of our lives are nonsense. When I was in high school, I had a fabulous teacher who would always call us on our "stuff." Having offered my excuse for being late, not having done my homework, missing practice, or any other number of infractions against his well-ordered universe, my teacher would say, "That sounds like excellent nonsense, Mr. Kelly." The implication was that no matter how well you articulate nonsense it is still nonsense. Even excellent nonsense remains nonsense.

Our lives have become full of excellent nonsense. It is time to take a wide-eyed, unflinching look at the nonsense that fills our lives.

The excessive haste, the constant state of urgency, and the incessant low-grade agitation are not serving us. The demands for greater speed, never-ending increases in efficiency, and blind obedience to busy all need to be put in their place. And the three-headed inner tyrant—fear, inadequacy, and shame—needs to be tamed.

It is time to slow down.

An unflinching, wide-eyed look at the nonsense that fills our lives will also lead us to the supreme truth that sits patiently at the center of our discussion: A life dominated by urgent, busy, and hurry is incompatible with the health and well-being of the human person, and incompatible with the things we say matter most.

Take relationships as an example. Love says: "I see you. I hear you. I am with you. I care. Rest a while. You are safe here with me. You are worthy."

This cannot be rushed.

We say we want love but refuse to slow our lives to a speed conducive to love.

It's time to take back our lives. Take a wide-eyed look at the nonsense that fills your life. If you have the courage to do that, today will be the beginnings of a glorious and deeply personal revolution. And keep in mind, a revolution, by definition, means to forcibly overthrow something.

So, let's be clear: Busy is the root cause of the inhumane speed of our lives. Busy will not depart from your life when politely asked. Urgent will not voluntarily stop screaming at you throughout the day. To establish the speed of joy in your life you will need to forcibly remove busy and urgent from your life.

Busy is a choice. Hurry is a choice. Don't make the mistake of thinking you have no choice. Don't surrender your power like that. Anytime you want to, you can abolish urgent, busy, and hurry from your life. It may take some time to fully establish the speed of joy, but you can get started today.

We may convince ourselves that our busy is necessary and unavoidable. That isn't true, at least not entirely. We are much busier than we need to be. For decades retired people have been saying, "I'm busier than ever since I retired." Now, children are overwhelmed by busy schedules that mirror their parents' fast-paced lives. Research by the Children's Hospital of Orange County found that 24% of children feel "too busy all the time" and 61% "wish they had more time." Children who are overscheduled are experiencing anxiety, fatigue, headaches, stomachaches, sleep issues, and depression. Busy is hurting everyone.

If the things we believe we must do are the consequences of past choices, it may be time for some new choices.

Busy is a choice and it's a bad choice. It's a choice I have made too many times. I was an overachiever when it came to choosing busy. The brutal truth is I spent most of my life in a mad rush. I completely swallowed the busy pill. I overdosed on busy. It was bad for me. It destroyed many relationships. In hindsight I am aware that the sheer speed and busyness of my life led me to hurt people. I didn't mean to hurt them. It wasn't intentional, but I doubt that made it hurt any less. My obsession with busy also mortgaged my health, and I am paying that mortgage now. The truth is busy almost killed me more than once.

When I am writing, I look up the definitions of dozens of words. I know what the words mean, but their formal definitions often shine unexpected light on the topic. The definition of busy is "having a great deal to do." But what struck me was the sentence they used as an example: "He was too busy to enjoy himself." That was me. I was that man.

Busy prevents us from enjoying the things we are doing. The more we try to cram into our days, the faster we tend to move through life. This is the relationship between busy and the speed of our lives. Busyness is the impetus for the speed of our lives, and therefore, the cause of our lost joy.

The faster you go the less you see. Go fast enough and everything becomes a blur. Does your life ever feel like one big blur? The faster you go the more likely you are to crash. People's lives are crashing. Relationships are crumbling, careers are collapsing, personal finances are unraveling, and everywhere we turn, we hear about physical and mental health breakdowns. What aspect of your life is most likely to crash if you increase the speed of your life?

The speed of our lives prevents us from recognizing the subtlety of human emotion in the people around us. The tone of someone's voice can signal she is having a rough day. A person's body language can reveal some unnamed suffering. A decrease in a child's appetite can communicate he is being bullied or abused. Someone you love has unmet and unspoken needs. But it is impossible to notice these things when our lives are moving too quickly, so people have to scream to get our attention.

What will it take to get your attention?

A MUTUAL TOXIC FRIEND

Most of us have experienced a toxic friendship. It takes time to identify it for what it is, but some people are like clouds—it's a beautiful day when they disappear. It takes time to extricate ourselves from these situations, but as a result, we now know a toxic friendship when we see one.

A toxic friendship is a relationship that disrupts your happiness and equilibrium by consistently negatively impacting your emotional and psychological health. Here are some signs you are in a toxic relationship:

It's always stressful or chaotic.

Constant negativity.

They are constantly critical of you.

Disrespect for your boundaries.

Lack of empathy and support.

Manipulative behavior.

Frequent conflict.

Unreliable.

Mean, degrading, abusive, or bullying.

They isolate you.

You feel physically and emotionally drained after spending time with them.

You find yourself losing sleep over the relationship.

They make promises they have no intention of keeping.

They encourage you to participate in behaviors that are risky or outright bad for you.

You cannot trust the person.

They never apologize.

The relationship is out of balance due to an imbalance of effort.

Diminished self-confidence and self-esteem.

They selfishly demand their wants be prioritized over your needs.

You catch yourself blaming yourself for their behavior.

Other important relationships suffer because of this relationship.

They never consider what is best for you.

The drama never stops.

You feel trapped.

# # #

If I had a friend who behaved in these ways you would encourage me to move on from that relationship. Well, it turns out we have a mutual toxic friend who is abusing us and ruining our lives in the same ways.

Busy is not your friend. It makes you feel overwhelmed, tired, and inadequate.

If busy were a person, would you spend all day with that person today, and then all day with that person again tomorrow? I doubt it. Not if you felt like you had a choice.

Busy isn't your friend. Judge the tree by its fruits and that becomes clear. The fruits of busy are overwhelmed, weary, tired, worn-out, resentful, discouraged, stressed, anxious, and burned out. Which of these fruits do you want in your life?

Researchers ask people every year, "What one word would you use to describe how you feel on a daily basis?" *Overwhelmed* is now the most common answer. Feeling overwhelmed has aggressively risen to the top of millions of people's list of dominant emotions over the past twenty years.

How often do you feel overwhelmed? Do you feel like there aren't enough hours in the day to get everything done? Are you overwhelmed with things that really matter or things that won't mean anything to anyone a month from now? Do you even have time to think?

We all know the feeling of exhaustion at the end of a day when you have worked hard on the right things—things that really matter. There is satisfaction in that tiredness. But we also know the exhaustion that comes from doing lots of nothing important. This exhaustion is heavy, draining, and meaningless.

When we are overwhelmed with things that we know don't really matter, we become resentful. So, it's not just that we are busy, but that we are busy with the wrong things.

Busy leads to overwhelmed, overwhelmed leads to weary, weary leads to discouraged, and discouragement leads us to feel resentful and inadequate. Anyone or anything that makes you feel that way is too small for you.

It is time to eradicate busy from our lives. Busy doesn't care about you. It doesn't care how much sleep you got last night. Busy doesn't care about your health, and it never factors in your relationships. Busy doesn't care about what is fair or reasonable. Busy creates unrealistic expectations and fills you with doubts and fears. It treats you like a machine because it has no soul.

Busy lacks all the essential qualities of a good friend. Busy is not your friend, it is an unjust and uncaring tyrant. Keep that in mind next time you feel pressured to say yes when you know you should say no. Remember that next time you feel tempted to add one more soul-destroying activity to your schedule.

Busy is loveless and lifeless and soulless, and so, it is completely incapable of knowing your hopes, hurts, needs, and dreams.

It is time to ruthlessly eliminate busy from our lives.

BUSY IS NOT A NEW PROBLEM

We are too busy. Most of us are at least vaguely aware of the negative impact busyness is having upon us. Yet, we seem content to continue along this destructive path.

And the problem of busy isn't a new one. Busy is not a modern phenomenon. Technology may have exponentially increased the insanity of our busy lives, but it isn't altogether responsible for the busy problem.

For thousands of years, voices from a cross-section of society have counseled us to avoid busyness, warned us of its ill effects on our bodies, hearts, minds, and souls, and encouraged us to vigorously guard our relationships and lives from its corrosive and destructive nature.

"Beware the barrenness of a busy life." —Socrates

"There is a pervasive form of modern violence. . . busy-ness. To allow oneself to be carried away by a multitude of conflicting concerns, to surrender to too many demands, to commit oneself to too many projects, to want to help everyone in everything, is to succumb to violence. The rush and pressure of modern life are a form, perhaps the most common form, of its innate violence." —Thomas Merton

"Busyness is not of the devil. It is the devil." —Carl Jung

"So many people walk around with a meaningless life. They seem half-asleep, even when they're busy doing things they think are important. This is because they're chasing the wrong things." —Morrie Schwartz

"Crazy-busy is a great way to stay numb. What a lot of us do is that we stay so busy, and so out in front of our life, that the truth of how we're feeling can't catch up. We stay busy so the truth of our lives can't catch up." —Brené Brown

"Busyness is the enemy of spirituality. It is essentially laziness. It is doing the easy thing instead of the hard thing." —Eugene Peterson

"Busy is the new stupid." —Warren Buffett

"Being busy is not the same as being productive. Often, busyness is nothing more than a form of mental laziness." —Elizabeth Gilbert

"It is not that we have a short time to live, but that we waste a lot of it. Life is long enough, and a sufficiently generous amount has been given to us for the highest achievements if it were all well invested. But when it is wasted in heedless luxury and spent on no good activity, we are forced at last by death's final constraint to realize that it has passed away before we knew it was passing." —Seneca

"If you seek tranquility, do less. Or (more accurately) do what's essential—what the logos of a social being requires, and in the requisite way. Which brings a double satisfaction: to do less, better." —Marcus Aurelius

"A 'successful' life has become a violent enterprise. We make war on our own bodies, pushing them beyond their limits; war on our children because we cannot find enough time to be with them when they are hurt and afraid and need our company; war on our spirit because we are too preoccupied to listen to the quiet voices that seek to nourish and refresh us." —Wayne Muller

"Most of us spend too much time on what is urgent and not enough time on what is important." —Stephen R. Covey

Busy doesn't make us important, it makes us unloving, ineffective, overwhelmed, distracted, exhausted, anxious, resentful, unfulfilled, inflexible, reactive, unhealthy, short-tempered, arrogant, and disconnected.

Busy is bad. This is a message that has rung out loud and clear for thousands of years, and yet, we are ignoring this wisdom today more than ever before.

A BRIEF HISTORY OF BUSY

Why are we all so busy? In order to fully understand the problem we are discussing, and seeking to solve, it is necessary to learn how we got to where we are today. *Why are we all so busy?* is a question worthy of reflection from three perspectives: the history of busyness, the general state of busyness in our society, and your own deeply personal answer to the question.

One reason it is crucial to explore the history of busyness is because we are now living in the future that was predicted to be less busy. More than predictions, these were the promises made in selling us on technology and other hallmarks of progress over the past three hundred years.

Another reason to understand the history of busyness is because there is a tendency to scapegoat work for the busyness of our lives. And what we will discover here is both fascinating and fixable.

Our briefest history of busyness begins with our ancient ancestors on the savanna. Dynamic biological and evolutionary forces were acting on our ancestors and continue to be significant forces within us today.

The mere quest to survive required a daily struggle for the earliest human beings. Our ancestors were constantly facing challenges that threatened their very existence. Their daily struggle to survive included finding sufficient food, adapting to changing environments, and avoiding or fighting off predators.

In *Idleness Aversion and the Need for Justifiable Busyness*, author Christopher K. Hsee and his co-authors observed, "In their strife for survival, human ancestors had to conserve energy to compete for scarce resources; expending energy without purpose could have jeopardized survival. With modern means of production, however, most people today no longer expend much energy on basic survival needs, so they have excessive energy, which they like to release through action."

In the December 2014 issue, *The Economist* observed, "Writing in the first century, Seneca was startled by how little people seemed to value their lives as they were living them—how busy, terribly busy, everyone seemed to be, mortal in their fears, immortal in their desires and wasteful of their time. He noticed how even wealthy people hustled their lives along, ruing their fortune, anticipating a time in the future when they would rest. 'People are frugal in guarding their personal property; but as soon as it comes to squandering time they are most wasteful of the one thing in which it is right to be stingy,' he observed in *On the Shortness of Life*, perhaps the very first time-management self-help book. Time on Earth may be uncertain and fleeting, but nearly everyone has enough of it to take some deep breaths, think deep thoughts and smell some roses, deeply. 'Life is long if you know how to use it,' he counseled."

From there we will leap forward to the eighteenth century. The Industrial Revolution brought about enormous changes in society and set the stage for the massive technological advancements of the nineteenth and twentieth centuries.

Machines played a central role. Mechanization of production gave birth to the mass production of goods and gave rise to the middle class. The speed of production compared to manual labor was dizzying.

This is when work was first synchronized with the clock, and so, this is when time became money. "How do you *spend* your time?" is a common question today, but before the Industrial Revolution people never thought of *spending* time.

"Once hours are financially quantified, people worry more about wasting, saving, or using them profitably. When economies grow and incomes rise, everyone's time becomes more valuable. And the more valuable something becomes, the scarcer it seems" (*The Economist*).

The efficiencies and economies of scale that machinery made possible led to the lines becoming blurred between the efficiency of a machine and the efficiency of a human being. Humanity developed an inferiority complex at this moment in history. Machines could work twenty-four hours a day. Human beings could not. The quest for efficiencies in machines was quickly transferred into a desire for increased human efficiency. There was one obvious problem: human beings are not machines. This is a truth that we often forget in the way we treat ourselves, and this forgotten truth leads to a busyness that is inhumane.

It wasn't long before economists and philosophers began predicting people would work much shorter hours in the future.

In 1930, the British economist John Maynard Keynes predicted technological advancements would lead to shorter working hours. In his essay *Economic Possibilities for Our Grandchildren*, Keynes speculated that within one hundred years, we would work three-hour shifts and fifteen hours a week. He believed that economic growth and efficiency gains would reduce the need for long working hours, giving people more time for leisure and creative pursuits.

In 1932, the philosopher Bertrand Russell wrote his essay In *Praise of Idleness* and predicted a twenty-hour work week. He argued that if society managed its resources and technological advancements properly, it could afford to significantly reduce working hours, leading to more leisure time and a higher quality of life. Russell was critical of the idea that constant work was a moral virtue and believed that more leisure time would benefit both individuals and society.

In 1948, the mathematician and philosopher Norbert Wiener, in his book *Cybernetics*, discussed the impact of automation on society. Wiener warned that while machines could lead to greater efficiency and productivity, there was also the potential for significant social disruption if the benefits were not shared equitably. He suggested that automation could reduce the need for human labor, potentially leading to reduced working hours, but also highlighted the risks of unemployment and inequality.

In 1959, Peter Drucker, the Austrian-born American management consultant, who is often referred to as the father of modern management, introduced the concept of the knowledge worker in his book *The Landmarks of Tomorrow*. Drucker painted a picture of the modern economy where the majority of employees were not manual laborers using their physical skills, but knowledge workers using their intellectual abilities to generate value through problem-solving, critical thinking, and creativity.

In the 1960s, the American architect and futurist Buckminster Fuller advocated that technological advancements would reduce the need for human labor. But unlike Keynes and Russell, who advocated radically reducing the number of hours worked, Fuller envisioned near-total automation to free people from the need to work extensively at all. He believed that automation and machinery would eventually handle most of the tasks that humans had to do, leading to a world where people worked less and focused more on creative and intellectual pursuits.

In 1967, Peter Drucker would further observe, in his book *The Effective Executive*, "One cannot buy, rent, or hire more time. The supply of time is totally inelastic. No matter how high the demand, the supply will not go up. There is no price for it. Time is totally perishable and cannot be stored. Yesterday's time is gone forever and will never come back. Time is always in short supply. There is no substitute for time. Everything requires time. All work takes place in and uses up time. Yet most people take for granted this unique, irreplaceable, and necessary resource."

In 1964, *The New York Times* science fiction writer Isaac Asimov predicted that by the year 2014, advancements in technology and automation would result in a society where people worked fewer hours and enjoyed more leisure time. He imagined a world where robots and computers would take over many jobs. Like Keynes and Russell, he predicted a twenty-hour work week.

These predictions reflect a long-standing belief that technological progress would eventually lead to a reduction in the need for human labor, allowing for more leisure and a higher quality of life. While some aspects of these predictions have come true, particularly in terms of productivity gains, the expected reduction in working hours has not materialized to the extent predicted by these thinkers.

One factor none of these writers foresaw or accounted for in their predictions was the staggering rise of materialism and consumerism. These attitudes, behaviors, and priorities led people to trade time for money in order to buy more things in an unprecedented way. These purchases were not the needs and modest wants that Keynes, Russell, and many others accounted for in their predictions. Our purchases have been of an ever-increasing discretionary and luxury nature. People one hundred years ago would consider the great majority of what middle-class Americans buy each year to be either luxuries or completely unnecessary (and in many cases both).

In 1965, Gary S. Becker had a series of interesting observations as noted here by *The Economist*, "The relationship between time, money and anxiety is something Gary S. Becker noticed in America's post-war boom years. Though economic progress and higher wages had raised everyone's standard of living, the hours of 'free' time Americans had been promised had come to naught. 'If anything, time is used more carefully today than a century ago,' he noted in 1965. He found that when people are paid more to work, they tend to work longer hours, because working becomes a more profitable use of time. So the rising value of work time puts pressure on all time. Leisure time starts to seem more stressful, as people feel compelled to use it wisely or not at all."

In 1971, Wayne Oates, the American psychologist, coined the term "workaholic" in his book *Confessions of a Workaholic*. Oates described a workaholic as someone who has an uncontrollable need to work incessantly and compared workaholism to an addiction to alcohol. The concept of workaholism has since become widely recognized and is often used to describe people who are excessively involved in work to the detriment of other aspects of their lives.

With the 1980s came the glorification of work, which brought us full circle. From the ancient civilizations of Greece and Rome, through Medieval Europe, to the Renaissance, the Enlightenment, the Industrial Revolution and Victorian England, leisure had always been a key marker of wealth and status. But toward the end of the twentieth century in the United States and beyond, work and busyness itself became a badge of honor. Work for the wealthy and elite had never been glorified in this way. The Protestant work ethic had been preached to the working class since the sixteenth century, and the key elements of this work ethic were: diligence, punctuality, deferment of gratification, and the primacy of work. But this was different. This wasn't the working class or even the middle class. This was the wealthy claiming excessive work and insanely busy lifestyles as a status symbol. This is when it became cool to be busy.

A whole new round of predictions regarding shorter work weeks and reduced hours has been fueled by advancements in Artificial Intelligence (AI). These predictions have been put forward by influential figures and organizations, ranging from the World Economic Forum to Steve Cohen, hedge fund founder and owner of the New York Mets. But I very much doubt these will come to fruition, for the same reason nothing came of the predictions made by Keynes, Russell, and Wiener. We seem too willing to trade our time for money so we can buy more stuff that we don't need. So, if the proposition is a four-day work week or a 20% pay raise to keep working a five-day week, we will take the money.

This is a brief history of the forces and choices that brought about our current busyness epidemic. I mentioned earlier that we have a tendency to scapegoat work for the busyness of our lives, but I encourage you to resist that temptation. It would be a massive oversimplification and false to say, "Work is the problem. The answer is to work less." Working less may very well be part of the solution, but how much we work isn't the only problem.

The problem may not be that we are bringing our work home as much as it is we are bringing our *approach* to work home and applying it to other aspects of our lives. The methods and systems we apply to our work to gain efficiencies fail when we try to apply them to parenting, marriage, friendship, leisure, spirituality, and other areas of life.

Work is an important part of life, but treating other aspects of our lives like work in a quest to get more done is a fool's errand. Trying to have an efficient conversation with your fifteen-year-old daughter who has just been dumped by the love of her life has no chance of success.

Busy is a problem. It has accelerated the speed of our lives to the point of being inhumane, and so, we are led to conclude that busy is an enemy of joy.

THE BUSY WAR

You are at war with busy. This may seem like an exaggeration, but if it isn't already, it will soon become staggeringly clear. If you don't realize this is a war, busy is probably obliterating you in each daily battle. What's at stake? If you don't win this war, the costs are both easy to imagine and impossible to fathom. So, let's explore a strategy that will help you win the war against busy, and let's discuss the reasons people lose the busy war.

History is full of examples of leaders and nations who refused to admit war was inevitable. It is also filled with examples of people who thought they could negotiate with lunatics who had their dark hearts set on war. If the world was full of sane and reasonable people, peace would always be the preferred option. But we have to live in the world as it is, not as we wish it were.

If you have anything worth having, sooner or later somebody is going to try to take it from you. You cannot subscribe to peace at any price. This is true for a nation, in relationships, when parenting, and it is true in your battle with busy.

Many of us are conflict-averse. We prefer to navigate through life with as little conflict as possible. This strategy may seem moderately successful until we discover how much residual resentment has built up in our hearts.

We prefer peace to conflict because we are lazy, afraid, and forget what is at stake. This leads us to attempt to negotiate with the insane and unreasonable. For example, if you find yourself in a relationship with an addict or a narcissist—personally or professionally—peace at all costs will lead to your demise.

Busy is irrational, unreasonable, and insane. It is incapable of morality because it has no soul. It cannot be appeased. If you want to thrive, war with busy is inevitable. The only question that remains is whether you will win the war. But to be clear, if you are wondering what is at stake, if you don't win, busy will obliterate you and everything that matters most to you.

When Adolf Hitler first came on the scene most people didn't take him seriously. They waved him off as an eccentric and got on with their lives. It is always a grave mistake not to take our enemies seriously, but such a mistake is inevitable when we foolishly believe we have no enemies.

A decade later, when it became clear that Hitler and the Nazis were going to be a problem far beyond Germany, Prime Minister Chamberlain naively tried to reason with Hitler. Chamberlain was blinded by his desire for peace. But our enemies lie and manipulate with every breath, and you cannot negotiate peace with an enemy that desires war above all else.

Winston Churchill saw Adolf Hitler for what he was long before most. He demanded that the Nazi threat be taken seriously, considered the peace-at-any-price idea to be cowardice, and was determined not to rest until Hitler and the Nazis had been defeated. Churchill knew one fundamental truth: You cannot reason with those who are unreasonable.

War is inevitable if you want to escape the joyless urgency. The truth is, you are already at war with busy, you have been at war with busy for a long time, and busy is opposed to almost everything you value most.

Once you realize war is inevitable, your mind can turn to winning the war. Your mind naturally begins searching for strategies that will maximize your chances of victory once you acknowledge that you are at war. But if you keep pretending that you are not at war, and that you can live peaceably with a lunatic, you will be obliterated.

The following is a simple guide to winning a war. It was written by Peter Kreeft, a Professor of Philosophy at Boston College, and will serve us powerfully in our war against busy by providing a blueprint for victory.

"To win any war, the three most necessary things to know are:
1. that you are at war
2. who your enemy is, and
3. what weapons or strategies can defeat that enemy.

You cannot win a war if:
1. you simply sew peace banners on a battlefield,
2. you fight civil wars against your allies, or
3. you use the wrong weapons and strategies."

You are at war. This is the brutal truth. No matter how unpalatable we may find it, this truth will not change. Your enemy is busy. This book will provide you with the weapons and strategies to defeat busy.

The easiest way to lose a war is to pretend you are not at war. This is why most people are losing their battle with busy. They have never considered the possibility that busy is a fierce enemy. They refuse to acknowledge that busy is diametrically opposed to what matters most. They foolishly try to reason with the insanity of busy. And they continue to believe that failed strategies like time management and prioritization can increase their efficiency and effectiveness and make busy irrelevant.

The will to fight comes from being clear about what's at stake. Busy is an enemy to your physical health, personal finances, marriage, parenting, career, spirituality, peace of mind, mental health, and so much more. And busy cannot be reasoned with. It will destroy you unless you actively subdue it in your life.

Busy isn't going to quietly vacate your life. Joyless urgency will remain the status quo unless you decide to wrestle with busy and win.

The ruthless elimination of busy is necessary to slow down and live at the speed of joy. But that means it's time for war.

# # #

This is what's going to happen next.

You will start slowing down to the speed of joy. You have probably already begun. There is something about the concept that is so powerful that simply becoming aware of it provides a new lens to see life through. It's invigorating, energizing, and hope-filled.

Slowing down to the speed of joy will release a whole range of emotions. You will feel a profound sense of relief. You will develop an inner calm despite the pressures and demands of daily life. Your awareness will increase. Things you would have previously overlooked will come into focus. New possibilities will begin to bubble up inside you. You will become excited about your future.

You will find yourself thinking more, reflecting on your life. Who am I? Who do I feel called to become? Big questions like these won't feel intimidating. Clarity will emerge. You will see your goals and values more clearly than you have in a long time. You will have questions. Be patient with your questions.

You may experience some anxiety and regret over aspects of life you have neglected. Acknowledge these and then set your worry aside. This is natural and normal.

The stress and tension of life in this busy world will begin to dissipate. You will find yourself spending more time doing the things that matter most and bring you joy. You will have moments of unbridled gratitude and contentment. You may experience a creative burst. And you will have more physical energy.

All of this will give birth to a new hope. Hope that a new beginning is possible. Hope that it isn't too late for you. Hope that something wonderful is about to happen. Hold onto that, because hope is precious, and you will need it along the way. Mary Ann Evans observed, "It is never too late to be what you might have been." I have always loved that idea.

Colonel Sanders was 62 when he opened his first Kentucky Fried Chicken franchise. Vera Wang worked as a journalist before becoming a fashion designer at the age of 40. The legendary Julia Child didn't learn to cook until she was 31 and didn't publish her first cookbook until she was 49. The billionaire Taikichiro Mori was an economics professor before leaving academia at age 55 to become a real estate investor. Morgan Freeman was 52 before he got a break in the movies.

We are about to explore what enables human beings to flourish, so this would be a fine time to do a little dreaming. Our ability to dream is often stifled by the busyness of life in the modern world. Slow down and dream a little. "It is never too late to be what you might have been." Ponder that idea in your heart. Or perhaps some new vision is emerging for your life. What hopes and dreams are surfacing in your heart at this time?

PART TWO

HUMAN
FLOURISHING

THE TRAIL ABOVE THE CLOUDS

One hundred years ago, an archeologist and his team set off to explore Machu Picchu and the ancient civilization of the Inca in South America. They arrived in Lima, Peru on a steamship, and then traveled by bus to Cusco, the former capital of the Inca, where they paused for three days to adjust to the altitude.

From there they traveled on a wagon drawn by mules while their equipment was carried by llamas to Piscacucho. They were now high in the Andes Mountains.

After years of planning and months of travel they were so close to their destination. Machu Picchu was now only twenty-eight miles away, but it was a treacherous twenty-eight miles that had claimed many lives.

Located high in the Andes of Peru, the ancient citadel of Machu Picchu was built for the Inca emperor Pachacuti in the fifteenth century. It is one of the most spectacular wonders of the world and is believed to have been a royal retreat or a sacred religious site.

That night our archeologist lay awake thinking about the first time he read the issue of *National Geographic* that detailed the American explorer Hiram Bingham's discovery of this lost city of the Incas in 1911. He must have read that issue a hundred times as a child. He had been dreaming of visiting ever since.

And now he was so close.

The archeologist spent the next day talking to locals about guides and porters. Who were the best? Which had the most experience? Could any speak English? Late that afternoon he settled on a team of guides and porters, negotiated rates of pay, and agreed that they would set out at sunrise the next morning.

Although they were a mere twenty-eight miles from the iconic ruins of Machu Picchu, it would take at least five days, the guides had explained. The archeologist knew this, but he had studied the route and believed it could be done in three days.

Machu Picchu is nestled in the Andes mountains at 7,972 feet above sea level. But in order to reach it you have to climb to Warmi Wañuska at 13,828 feet before descending to the lost city. This path is known today as The Inca Trail.

That evening he reviewed this final leg of the journey with his team and the guides.

The guides explained that the trail would immerse the archeologist and his team in stunning landscapes, from rainforests to vast open valleys, deep canyons to high plateaus, rugged mountain terrain to cloud forests. It was because of these cloud forests that the locals named it "the trail above the clouds."

But the guides also warned that for all its beauty, the last twenty-eight miles of their journey presented an endless array of danger. It was a high-altitude battle against slippery rocks and unpredictable weather. A single moment of distraction could be fatal.

There was also the risk of mountain sickness, which is brought on by rising and falling altitudes, and causes headaches, dizziness, shortness of breath, loss of energy, nausea, and vomiting. So, while this final stage of their journey was not very long it presented a myriad of challenges.

Along the way they would pass a handful of other ancient Inca ruins, but the archeologist had no intention of pausing to explore those.

At sunrise the next morning they set off. The archeologist immediately set such a grueling pace that even the guides struggled to keep up. His team and the porters trailed behind at a distance that increased with every passing hour.

As the sun began to set, the archeologist and the guides agreed on a camp site for the evening. Twilight brought some of the team and porters to camp, but it was dusk by the time the last arrived.

Around the campfire that night, the archeologist congratulated the team for making great progress, and explained that they were set up now to achieve his goal of arriving in Machu Picchu in three days rather than five.

Early the next morning the archeologist and his team were packed and ready to go, but the porters refused to break camp. There was arguing between the guides and the porters, but the visitors could not make out what the locals were saying to each other.

The guides walked away from the porters and huddled to discuss something among themselves, before returning to the porters. But the arguing immediately broke out again.

The chief guide finally approached the archeologist and pulled him aside from the rest of the group.

"We have a problem," he began.

"What sort of problem?" the archeologist asked.

"It's difficult to explain," the guide continued. "I suppose it would be considered a spiritual problem."

"A spiritual problem?" the archeologist exclaimed with bewilderment. "What kind of spiritual problem?"

"The porters refuse to move on. They say we must wait until tomorrow before we go any further."

"Tomorrow? That's absurd. Why?" the archeologist asked indignantly.

"They are afraid of. . ." the guide began to explain.

"Afraid of what?" the exasperated archeologist interrupted.

"They are afraid of losing their souls."

"How is that possible?" the archeologist asked, baffled and frustrated.

"We went so fast yesterday that we have to wait for our souls to catch up."

THE OPPOSITE OF BUSY

How far behind is your soul?

We are so disinterested in being anything other than busy that there isn't even a word for the opposite of busy in our common vernacular. This was a staggering discovery for me. I had never thought about it before.

Language is powerful. Words have an extraordinary impact on what we think and how we behave, both individually and as a whole society. A thesaurus will tell you the opposite of busy is unbusy, but I have never heard anybody use the word unbusy.

Think about that for a moment. The opposite of busy is so unimportant and so undesirable that we haven't even assigned it a word in the language we use every day.

It is also significant that the antonyms of busy are largely derogatory. Language also provides a unique window into what a culture values. Our radical cultural bias toward busy is displayed in its antonyms: idle, inactive, lazy, dormant, and passive. Nobody wants to be labeled idle, inactive, lazy, dormant, and passive. The language itself is a deterrent to living our lives at a sane and reasonable speed. So even when people aren't busy, they often pretend to be busy.

The contrast between the derogatory and undesirable antonyms of busy and the synonyms of busy is also worth noting. The synonyms of busy are positive and desirable: engaged, diligent, industrious, and active. It is easy to see how language itself can create a type of silent cultural peer pressure.

We encounter a similar and perhaps more egregious situation as we explore the opposite of fast. The opposite of fast is slow. This alone carries a significant amount of cultural negativity. To be considered slow is to be considered ignorant, stupid, brainless, unintelligent, dense, dimwitted, or someone who takes a long time to understand things.

Synonyms for slow can be broken into two groups. The first group demonstrates in part what we are striving for and includes: unhurried, leisurely, diligent, measured, steady, moderate, relaxed, unrushed, gentle, and thoughtful. The second group contains today's culture's opinion of slow: dull-witted, unperceptive, lax, lethargic, sluggish, stagnant, uncomprehending, and inert.

All this leads to a crucial piece of information we need to understand if we are going to live at the speed of joy. The speed of joy is *not* the opposite of fast, and it *isn't* the opposite of busy.

We are not striving for the opposite of busy or the opposite of fast. We are striving for something altogether different.

Our minds think: *There must be an ideal state between busy and idle. There must be a state that allows human beings to thrive, an optimum state for human beings, a state that best facilitates human flourishing.*

There is such a state, but it isn't found between busy and idle, and it isn't the opposite of fast or busy. The ideal state that most encourages people to flourish contains intense activity and idleness, and everything in between; it contains fast and slow, and every state in between. It also includes states that are not in between fast and slow, but are essential to human flourishing: pause and stop.

The speed of joy isn't one speed. It isn't one static level of activity. It requires the human heart and mind to discern what is best for each season of life, for each day and week, and for each activity each day.

I know how disappointing this will be to some and frustrating to others. Somewhere deep inside we all want someone to tell us the speed of joy is X, so we can set our lives on cruise control and attempt to live at that one speed. But it is more complicated and wonderful than that, and thank God it is, because that one elusive speed would become awfully dull before too long.

Taking your time to do something properly—that is wisdom. That's what we are striving for in our quest to live at the speed of joy. The speed of joy is deliberate, intentional, and diligent. It may be fast at times; it may be slow at times. The speed of joy can include intense activity and great accomplishment.

Think about a mother of young children. She is almost constantly engaged in intense activity and demanding tasks, but she can approach her day with a calm or frenzied attitude. The speed of joy is as much about this inner attitude as it is about the amount of activity on our schedule.

Parents can, however, wake up to the cultural insanity of children participating in eighty-seven extracurricular activities at the same time. Running around in a clump of tiny humans chasing a ball isn't a fundamental rite of passage. Learning to gracefully introduce macaroni, glitter, and glue isn't an essential life skill.

"What activities are your little ones doing?" I've learned never to ask the question, because if you do, this is what the answers sound like: Soccer, piano lessons, karate, art classes, gymnastics, swimming lessons, ballet, chess club, drama club, science club, baseball, tennis lessons, basketball, golf, hockey, Lego-robotics, Scouts, ice-skating, violin, extreme napping, cloud watching club, sock sorting Olympics, pet rock caretaking, invisible orchestra, dirt sculpture class, procrastination practice, bubble wrap popping therapy, couch fort architecture, synchronized screaming, snack art, select puddle jumping, advanced hide-and-seek ninja training. . . okay, I just started making them up. But that's what it sounds like, and I have to keep myself from laughing and crying at the same time.

Parents can limit the number of activities their children participate in, and they should. Not limiting the number of activities our children participate in is setting them up for the insanity we are trying to correct by slowing down to the speed of joy.

Parents of young children can live at the speed of joy. There are unique challenges, but it is possible. One of the main lessons for parents is: Be careful not to self-inflict too much unnecessary activity upon yourself, your children, and your family. There is plenty of necessary activity and unavoidable unnecessary activity.

A mother of young children, an executive of a large company, a nurse in an emergency room, a professional athlete, a schoolteacher, a chef running a busy kitchen, a research scientist. . . the speed of joy is available to them all.

Slowing down to the speed of joy isn't just about removing things from our to-do lists. It's about establishing and maintaining an internal disposition of calm joy. Mother Teresa accomplished a great deal every day, but she was a fountain of joy to everyone everywhere she went, and her ability to give each person her wholehearted attention was legendary.

The distinction between intense activity and mere busyness is this: When we are living at the speed of joy we can fully engage in demanding tasks while preserving inner calm and growing more aware of the needs of others.

You can accomplish a great deal in a day and still live at the speed of joy. And the speed of joy is never an excuse to be lazy.

The speed of joy is wise and adaptable. It mindfully selects the speed most appropriate for the task at hand. The speed of joy is the ideal speed for each activity.

There are times when the most appropriate speed is "with all haste." Mary went with all haste to serve her cousin Elizabeth (Luke 1:39). When a mother is in labor her husband drives to the hospital with all haste. Abraham hurried to serve his guests (Genesis 18). If there is a fire you evacuate the building with all haste. The Israelites are instructed to eat the Passover meal in haste as they are about to leave Egypt (Exodus 12:11). If you have hurt another person with your words, actions, or inaction, you act swiftly to apologize. The angels urged Lot to hurry out of Sodom because it was about to be destroyed (Genesis 19). If you discover you transferred money to the wrong account, you act quickly to rectify your error. Jesus tells Zacchaeus the tax collector to hurry down from the tree because he is going to stay at his house (Luke 19:5-6). If you notice a child is in danger, you act without hesitation to remove them from harm.

The speed of joy is desirable, but mere busyness and speed are impediments to the speed of joy, and so we need to overcome our addiction to busy and speed.

Busy drives speed. This is how they relate to each other. If your pile of things to do wasn't so massive you would live your life at a more humane pace. Busy drives speed. Speed is the drug, busy is the dealer, and we are addicted.

Take a moment to consider the effects of the street drug known as speed. It provides an adrenaline rush that increases activity, induces talkativeness, produces faster and shallower breathing, elevates blood pressure, and triggers a rapid heart rate. It may also make you feel nervous, agitated, and aggressive, can cause confusion, paranoia, and depression, and increases the risk of heart attack.

The speed of modern life appears to have many of the same effects on us.

THERE MUST BE A BETTER WAY

The busyness of our lives leaves us feeling anxious, overwhelmed, exhausted, stressed-out, worn-out, resentful, discouraged, and inadequate—and the speed of our lives multiplies these feelings. There must be a better way.

Albert Einstein observed, "Look deep, deep into nature, and then you will understand everything better." So, let's begin our pursuit of a better way by looking deep, deep into nature.

What does nature teach us about how to live?

There is a natural rhythm to life. Every element of creation is in harmony with that rhythm when it is healthy.

Your heart beats to a rhythm, pumping blood around your body, carrying oxygen to every cell.

Your brain has an internal twenty-four-hour clock known as circadian rhythm which regulates cycles of alertness and sleepiness.

Our bodies have a second internal clock known as infradian rhythm which regulates biological cycles that last longer than twenty-four hours. This infradian rhythm governs the menstrual cycles in a woman's body that play a powerful role in reproduction. The rhythm brings forth life.

The birds of the air and the fish of the sea depend on the rhythm of life pumping through their veins.

The rhythm of life synchronizes the process of photosynthesis which is essential to the growth, development, and fruition of plants.

The stars and the planets align with the rhythm through time.

The seasons have their cycles—the darkness, death, and cold of winter give way to the warmth, joy, and new life of spring.

The sun rises in the east, flooding the world with the light of a new day, and then at the end of each day, surrenders to the darkness of the night as it sets in the west.

The waves fall upon the beach and the tides come in and go out attuned to the rhythm.

Creation is ordered by rhythm.

Each aspect of creation thrives when it abides by the rhythm, but when we lose the rhythm of life, chaos and destruction quickly begin to reign.

We make dozens of choices every day. Each choice aligns us with the rhythm of life or destroys the rhythm of our lives.

We have all witnessed how disagreeable small children become if their daily routines and rituals are disrupted.

What happens when your circadian rhythm is out of sync? This can lead to daytime sleepiness, decreased alertness, memory problems, irritableness, difficulty making decisions, and poor decisions.

What happens if your heart falls out of rhythm? This is known as arrhythmia and can cause brain damage. It can also lead to stroke, cardiac arrest, and heart failure, all of which can be fatal.

We have lost the rhythm of life, but we can get it back. The first step is to slow down.

What would happen if you tried to run a marathon like it were a 100-meter dash? That's what we are doing. Life is a marathon, not a 100-meter sprint.

As we slow down clarity begins to emerge and we see the insanity of our lives, but we also see a more ennobling path before us.

The speed of joy and the rhythm of life are in perfect harmony.

The speed of joy honors our legitimate needs—physically, emotionally, intellectually, and spiritually. It is the perfect combination of rest, leisure, and activity at the optimal pace. Find the speed of joy and it will flood your life with energy, enthusiasm, and creativity.

The speed of our lives is not aligned with our hopes, dreams, values, and priorities. The joyless urgency that is dominating our culture leads us to realize that the speed and busyness we have adopted cannot be how life was intended to be lived.

There must be a better way. What we are doing isn't working. The wisdom of nature makes this clear. But there is another reason that there simply must be a better way. This reason is indisputable. It is the great human mandate.

THE GREAT HUMAN MANDATE

Would it surprise you to discover that a great mandate has been placed upon your life?

Five years ago, when I began slowing down and trying to unravel the insanity of my own busy life, there was one realization that destroyed all my excuses and justifications. A great mandate has been placed on my life. That was the realization that created a moment of exceptional clarity.

The same great mandate has been placed on your life. What is a mandate? A mandate is a directive, issued by someone with due authority, that commands, instructs, or commissions a person to carry out a specific task, responsibility, or duty.

When I read this description of a mandate, I see so much of what our culture rejects, avoids, resists, and despises—authority, being told what to do, personal responsibility, and duty. It should therefore be no surprise we are struggling to live out the mandate.

Love is the mandate of my God. In a single quiet moment, sitting in my office at home, looking across the field, I was confronted by these uncomfortable truths: The speed of my life was incongruent with love, and the busyness of my life was incompatible with love.

What is the speed of love? What speed of life is most conducive to love and healthy relationships?

I know I haven't spent enough of my life at that speed.

You cannot hurry love. You can't multi-task love. Love cannot be hacked. It can't be scheduled. It can't be achieved on a predetermined time-frame and the idea of loving someone efficiently is ludicrous.

Love cannot be rushed. It takes as long as it takes. Love says: "I see you. I hear you. You are worthy. I am with you. I care. Rest a while. You are safe here with me. You are worthy." This cannot be rushed. I cannot see you and hear you in a hurry. I can't rush being with you or caring for you and call it love. I cannot impatiently lead you to believe you are safe.

When we are moving too fast, we don't notice the little things that love notices. A hesitant smile, a discouraged heart, other people's needs, a deflated tone in her voice, a longing to be held, the way a child hovers around when he wants to talk to you. There are so many things you can only see when you slow down. These are just a handful.

Love notices. Love pays attention. Speed and busy are obstacles to love. The more we add to our schedules the harder it becomes to love. The faster our lives become the more impossible it becomes to love.

Sometimes we pretend to be confused about what we should be doing with our lives, but at a foundational level the answer is clear. The details may be fuzzy, but the mandate is clear: love.

Jesus was teaching one day in the synagogue when he was asked, "Which is the greatest of the commandments?" The question was a trap. There were 613 Jewish commandments (Mitzvot in Hebrew) and each had been extracted from the Old Testament.

These laws were meant to protect people from breaking the Ten Commandments. But many Jewish people were so fixated on the laws that they lost sight of the central teaching of the Torah and the heart of God's message: love. It was easier to keep busy with the 613 and neglect God's mandate to love.

Jesus effortlessly avoids the trap and cuts through the complexity. With the power of clarity and the genius of simplicity, he answers the question and perfectly summarizes the Gospel.

"'Love the Lord your God with all your heart, with all your soul, and with all your mind.' This is the first and the greatest commandment. And the second is like it: 'Love your neighbor as yourself'" (Matthew 22:37-39).

In forty words Jesus gives us a guide to life. In forty words he gives us a mini-Gospel. In forty words he gives us an examination of conscience. In forty words he essentially says: If you are looking for something to measure your life by, use this!

The mandate is clear. Love is the mandate. But not just any kind of love. Not a love that is open to interpretation. No. The mandate is clear. Wholehearted love is the mandate. Love with all your heart, with all your soul, and with all your mind. Wholehearted love.

Sitting in my office that morning it was disturbingly clear that huge swaths of my life didn't measure up to those forty words.

It was disconcerting because I thought I had been dedicating my life to God. But it is easy to forget that Jesus didn't say. . . they will know you are Christian by the number of countries you visit to share the Good News, or by how many people attend your talks, seminars, and retreats. Jesus didn't say they will know you are Christian by how many books you write, or how many bestsellers you have, or how many millions of copies are sold. No. His prescription was clear, "They will know you are Christians by your love" (John 13:35).

The uncomfortable truth is that there have been many times in my life when I have been unrecognizable by Jesus' criteria. There have been too many times when nobody would have known I was a Christian by my love, because it was obscured and diminished by the speed and busyness of my life.

We find ourselves in a conundrum as modern Christians when it comes to the speed and busyness that dominate our lives. The speed of our lives is unchristian. The busyness of our lives is unchristian. They prevent us from fulfilling the great human mandate to love wholeheartedly.

Our faith is being completely undermined by the speed of our lives, the default speed and busyness of modern society, and the sheer busyness we have adopted for ourselves.

The speed and busyness of our lives is selfish, covetous, uncharitable, and faithless absurdity. Rather than conforming our lives to the teachings of Jesus, we are conforming our lives to the tyrants of modern secularism: urgent, busy, and hurry.

God's mandate is love. The speed of our lives is incompatible with love. The busyness of our lives is incompatible with love. This busyness is not of God. Our joyless urgency is not of God. We have brought this breathlessness upon ourselves, but we can choose a new path.

My mind is drawn to Cornelia ten Boom, a Dutch watchmaker who hid Jews and people with disabilities from Nazi persecution during World War II. She was ultimately arrested in February 1944 and sent to the Ravensbrück concentration camp, fifty miles north of Berlin. Corrie was released nine months after her arrest based on a clerical error. One week later the rest of the women in her group were sent to their deaths in the gas chambers.

After the war she returned to the Netherlands to open a rehabilitation center for concentration camp survivors. Twenty-five years later, at the age of eighty, she published her first book, and her quotes have been shared far and wide.

"Worry does not empty tomorrow of its sorrow, it empties today of its strength."

"Forgiveness is an act of the will, and the will can function regardless of the temperature of the heart."

"Every experience God gives us, every person He puts in our lives is the perfect preparation for the future that only He can see."

"If you look at the world, you'll be distressed. If you look within, you'll be depressed. If you look at God you'll be at rest."

"Is prayer your steering wheel or your spare tire?"

"Never be afraid to trust an unknown future to a known God."

"Worry is a cycle of inefficient thoughts whirling around a center of fear."

But her quote that my mind is drawn to in this moment is, "If the devil can't make us bad, he will make us busy."

Very few things benefit from being done quickly. Most things are worse off when we rush them. The speed of joy is about giving each task the time it needs to be done with excellence and joy.

We have embraced pathological busyness. We are rushing around, living lives of distraction, addicted to the urgent, perennially neglecting everything we claim is most important, unable to be present to the moment because we are preoccupied with the busyness that needs to be attended to next.

Most people can't even commit to one screen at a time, so the concept of being fully present to anyone or anything is increasingly foreign.

The speed and busyness of our lives stand in direct opposition to love. The speed of our lives is an enemy of what we say matters most.

Busy reduces our capacity to love. Busy is a destroyer of love. Busy robs us of so many opportunities to love and be loved. Busy dehumanizes people—ourselves and others—and the result of that dehumanization is a reduced capacity to love. Each dehumanizing experience diminishes our future capacity to love, and most of us have been dehumanized much more than we are aware. This downward cycle desperately needs to be broken and reversed. We need to slow down so we can learn to love again. We need to be rehumanized. This is the great task that sits on the threshold between humanity and the future we hope for.

Busy kills love. Ruthlessly eliminate busy from your life and you will discover an endless stream of opportunities to love. Love more each day and you will experience unimaginable happiness and fulfillment.

If love is the great mandate that has been placed upon our lives, why is our love so often absent or mediocre?

People pursue excellence in every field and discipline, and pride themselves on the excellence they achieve. Striving for excellence has been sewn into the fabric of our culture. But where are the people striving to be excellent at loving wholeheartedly? Have you ever made it a goal to become excellent at loving? And wouldn't it be a shame to pass through this world without ever making love the central focus of your life?

The first step is to slow down.

There is a better way to live. We don't have to remain trapped in the joyless urgency and frantic living that dominate our culture today. Our collective dissatisfaction suggests there must be a better way. Nature demonstrates there must be another way. The great human mandate demands that there must be a better way. Let's discover that better way together.

HUMAN FLOURISHING

Slowing down is not our goal. Our goal is human flourishing. Slowing down allows us to reconnect with our humanity—needs, talents, desires, hopes, fears and dreams—so that we can learn to flourish again.

What does it mean to flourish?

The Health Equity and Policy Lab at the University of Pennsylvania describes it in this way: "Human flourishing is the ability to live a good life. Rooted in Aristotelian ethics, it values health intrinsically and applies universally to all human lives. Human flourishing embraces our shared humanity and serves everyone's interest. All people should have the conditions for flourishing and realizing their ability to be healthy. They can use their values, talents, and abilities in pursuit of their own goals and health."

If you present people with the statement "All people should have the conditions for flourishing" and ask them who they believe is most at risk of not flourishing, they will probably identify people of poorer and developing countries along with those living in poverty in their own country. They would be right in one sense. But in another very real sense the people living in the most prosperous nations on earth are just as at risk of not flourishing.

Flourishing is "feeling good combined with functioning well," according to Corey Keyes, a sociologist and professor emeritus at Emory University. Are you flourishing?

The first definition Merriam-Webster gives for flourishing is "marked by vigorous and healthy growth" as in a flourishing garden. The second definition is "very active and successful" as in a flourishing career. It immediately occurred to me that both definitions would apply to very few people simultaneously. I don't know many people who are "very active and very successful," who are also "very healthy," if we account for all four aspects of the human person: physical, emotional, intellectual, and spiritual.

"Are you thriving or are you just surviving?" I wrote these words over twenty-five years ago and survivalism was rampant in our culture at that time. Most of the world's population is in survival mode.

Survivalism is a social movement made up of groups and individuals who proactively prepare for dangerous and unpleasant emergencies and disasters that will lead to a disruption of the social order caused by natural, economic, or political crisis. This is not the form of survivalism I speak of here. There is another type of survivalism that is dangerous, unpleasant, and a constant threat to our well-being and happiness, that most of us participate in all too willingly every day.

"I'm in survival mode," someone will say. Others nod their heads knowingly. But nobody rushes to do anything about it. Everyone just accepts it as part of modern existence.

I believe it's time we did something about it.

Ten years ago, two professors from the University of Cambridge, Felicia Huppert and Timothy So, conducted a research initiative to measure *flourishing* in twenty-three European nations, known as *The Flourishing Across Europe Study*. The country with the highest percentage of flourishing citizens was Denmark at 33%. The list of the top five nations was rounded out by Switzerland (26%), Finland (25%), Norway (24%), and Ireland (23%). These nations celebrated. What were they celebrating? How many of their citizens were flourishing? Not really. They were celebrating that more of their citizens were flourishing than other nations. If the research had been commissioned by a single nation, and the study had found that two out of every three Danish citizens were not flourishing, would there have been the same celebration? I think not.

What does it mean to flourish? How did these researchers answer our question? *The Flourishing Across Europe Study* used these ten markers to measure flourishing in their research:

Competence
Most days I feel a sense of accomplishment from what I do.
Emotional Stability
I felt calm and peaceful in the past week.
Engagement
I love learning new things.
Meaning
I generally feel that what I do in my life is valuable and worthwhile.
Optimism
I am optimistic about my future.
Positive Emotion
Taking all things together I am relatively happy.
Positive Relationships
There are people in my life who really care about me.
Resilience
When things go wrong in my life it generally doesn't take me long to get back to normal.
Self-esteem
I generally feel very positive about myself.
Vitality
I had a lot of energy in the past week.

These ten markers were divided into two categories: core features and additional features. Respondents were required to have all three core features and three of the additional seven features to be considered flourishing.

Core Features
    Positive Emotion
    Engagement
    Meaning

Additional Features
- Competence
- Emotional Stability
- Optimism
- Positive Relationships
- Resilience
- Self-esteem
- Vitality

There is no perfect measure of human flourishing, but I absolutely applaud the effort to measure well-being.

For too long nations have been satisfied measuring our "standard of living" with a single piece of data: economic growth (measured using Gross Domestic Product). The inference is that if the average household income is increasing, our standard of living is increasing. But there is a lot more to our standard of living than how much money we make and how much stuff we can buy.

Two Nobel Prize laureates, Daniel Kahneman and Angus Deaton, published a groundbreaking study in 2010 showing that a rise in income did increase people's well-being, but only up to a ceiling of $75,000, beyond which there was no increase in well-being. Adjusted for inflation, money stops increasing your happiness and well-being at $117,043 in 2024.

The limitations to the model above are similar to studies that only measured economic growth.

What was not included in this study? It would be easy to point out morality, spirituality, and ethics. These would no doubt spark debate, a debate that is worth having, but let us begin with less contentious topics. The absence of civic duty, or any duty for that matter, seemed ominous. The fact that the measure used for Positive Relationships was a one-way street was further concerning (*there are people in my life who really care about me*).

The markers used were completely self-referential. Under these guidelines, a person who was incredibly selfish could be ruled to be flourishing. A complete narcissist has a greater chance of being identified as flourishing under their criteria than the average person on the street.

None of the ten markers accounted for helping other people or service to strangers. And yet, it would seem to me that a leading indicator of a thriving person, relationship, family, society, and nation is found (at least in part) in our willingness to make personal sacrifices to help other people (especially those who cannot help themselves). How willing are you to go out of your way to help others? This is a core component of human flourishing.

# # #

When we are flourishing, we have abundant energy and enthusiasm for all that matters most, and all this makes us more aware of other people's needs and more willing to meet them. From our abundance (flourishing) we delight in sharing. But when we are in a state of scarcity (stress and anxiety) we are incapable of considering the needs of others because we are too focused on our own. Our capacity to love and honor the great human mandate expands the more we flourish.

Busy prevents us from flourishing. It is an obstacle to the fruits of flourishing: emotional well-being, happiness, joy, satisfaction, contentment, mental health, the ability to bounce back from adversity, a strong sense of self and your profound worthiness, positive relationships, strong social connections, the awareness and energy necessary for empathy and kindness, physical health, vitality and energy, a sense of your meaning and purpose, engagement at work, the ability to do your best work, creativity, innovation, openness to new ideas that are not your own, spiritual health, better decisions, the ability to identify enduring wisdom and apply it to your life. . . to name just a few. But busy is keeping us from flourishing, and by extension, keeping all of these elevating realities from filling our daily lives.

We are too busy for our own good. We know that. We don't want to be neglectful of our spouse's needs and impatient with our children. We don't want our professional work to be just good enough. We want to be more loving and generous. We do. But we lack the capacity to live this way because we're constantly rushing around in a frenzy doing too many things that matter too little.

At what speed do you flourish? Well, as we have briefly discussed already, it's a different speed in different situations. But if you take a moment to pause during the day and ask yourself if you are flourishing you will know immediately. If you are not, slow down. The speed of joy is the speed that allows you to flourish.

Reflecting on the speed and busyness of my own life was like sitting on a beach at high tide, one wave came crashing down upon me after another. This was the next crushing realization that came crashing down: I am at my worst when I am busy. And the busier I get the worse I get. This is when I make mistakes that become regrets.

How busy is too busy? That depends quite a bit on everything else that's happening in our lives at that time. You could be busy and flourishing, but your wife gets sick, you need to handle more at home, you start to get stressed, and things start to fall apart. This indicates we were too busy to start with. Life is full of unexpected eventualities. You could be busy and thriving, but then a client requests you work on a new project, the stress begins to build, the cracks begin to show, and your flourishing evaporates. What seems like a healthy and manageable amount of busy can quickly become overwhelming if a difficult time emerges in your child's life.

What is the ideal speed of life? The speed at which you can flourish. What is the right amount of busyness? The amount of activity that facilitates your flourishing.

JESUS WAS NEVER IN A HURRY

Those six words are worthy of some profound reflection. Jesus was never in a hurry. The three tyrants— urgent, busy, hurry—had no place in his life.

Jesus was never in a rush. He lived an unhurried life. He was a peaceful presence. He brought a calm to every room he entered. He was present to whoever was before him in that moment. He gave his wholehearted attention to the person he was with in the moment, he gave his whole self to whatever activity he was doing. If he was eating a meal with his disciples, he wasn't preoccupied with the next village they were going to visit. If he was talking to someone, he wasn't looking over their shoulder to see who else was there. He was where he was. And Jesus didn't hustle as fast as he could from one place to the next. He lived at a leisurely pace. He did everything wholeheartedly. He knew how much activity was enough for a single day.

Our lives seem to be the complete opposite. Urgent, busy, and hurry are often in control of our lives.

We are always in a rush.

We lived hurried lives.

We are a stressful presence. We bring chaos to the rooms we enter.

We are not present to the one person before us.

We give only halfhearted attention to the person before us in the moment.

We give only a portion of ourselves to anything.

If we are eating a meal with family or friends, we are preoccupied with our plans tomorrow or something that happened earlier today.

If we are talking to someone, we are looking over their shoulder to see who else is there.

We are always somewhere other than the now.

We are always hustling as fast as we can to get from one place to the next.

We are living our lives at an insane pace.

We do everything halfheartedly.

We have no sense of how much activity is enough for a single day.

#

Jesus was never in a physical hurry. There may have been times when he moved with a holy sense of haste to do the Father's will, but he never moved with the kind of frenzied panic that often defines our lives. His approach to life was calm, patient, and deliberate.

Take the healing of Lazarus as an example. When Jesus was informed that his friend was gravely ill, he didn't panic. He didn't rush. When he did arrive and found his friend was dead, again he remained calm (John 11:1-44).

Jesus often took time in quiet prayer. This is more proof that Jesus was never in a physical hurry. The crowds were constantly seeking him. The demands they made of him to teach them and heal them were unending, and yet Jesus often withdrew to a quiet place (Luke 5:16).

Even when he was walking on water, he wasn't in a frenzy because the disciples were in a frenzy. He walked calmly across the water (Mark 6:45-52).

Jesus was never in an emotional hurry. He was emotionally grounded, composed, and unrushed.

A striking example of Jesus' unhurried presence in emotional situations is the beautiful scene where the woman is weeping, allowing her tears to wash his feet, and drying his feet with her hair, before kissing his feet and anointing them with the ointment from the alabaster jar (Luke 7:36-50).

How would you have handled this situation? I know for certain I would have been uncomfortable in so many ways and would have been in a hurry for it to end.

It would have been easy for Jesus to say, "It's okay, there is no need to cry." We would have tried to comfort her in some way. But Jesus knew she needed to shed those tears and he was not going to interrupt. He had the patience to let it play out.

Would that be uncomfortable? Yes, I think so. Everyone watching, people talking behind your back, and all the thoughts racing through your mind. Yes, that would be uncomfortable. But learning to patiently allow uncomfortable situations to naturally unfold is essential to loving people.

Get comfortable being uncomfortable. This is a requirement of slowing down to the speed of joy. When we are uncomfortable and focus on that, we are focusing on ourselves rather than the needs of the person whose pain and suffering is no doubt more uncomfortable.

Another example of Jesus' emotional patience was in the Garden of Gethsemane the night before he died. We are told he was "deeply distressed and troubled" (Mark 14:32-42).

We are notorious for rushing through situations that make us uncomfortable. We end them prematurely. We try to completely avoid situations that trouble or distress us.

But Jesus spent three hours in that state. He went deep into his emotions. He wrestled with what was to come. He prayed and begged the Father to find another way. It took him three hours to reach a place of emotional, psychological, and spiritual acceptance.

We rarely experience this profound acceptance because we refuse to patiently sit with our troubles and distress. We avoid them. We hurry to get away from them. We rush to prematurely end any situation that gives rise to uncomfortable emotions.

Jesus was never in an intellectual hurry.

There are plenty of examples of Jesus' intellectual patience. We see it first when he is a child visiting Jerusalem and spends three days in the temple conversing with the priests and teachers (Luke 2:41-52).

But the most compelling example I find is his daily life with his disciples. He is there in their midst every day, and yet, over and over again they fail to grasp what he is saying to them. The disciples struggled to comprehend the fullness of Jesus' message, but Jesus was endlessly patient with them, often taking time to explain certain teachings and parables to them in private.

He feeds five-thousand people, but they are astonished to see him walking on water (Mark 6:35-52).

Peter tells Jesus he will never let him die in the manner Jesus is predicting (Matthew 16:21-28). He has failed to grasp the mission and vision Jesus has repeatedly shared with the disciples, but Jesus' patience with Peter is endless.

James and John request seats of honor (Mark 10:35-45). This is once again a clear sign that these brothers have failed to absorb Jesus' teaching.

The disciples' inability to comprehend the Master's parables (Matthew 13:10-17).

Jesus tells them over and again about his death and Resurrection, but they seem incapable of grasping what he is saying (Luke 18:31-34).

Peter, James, and John are incapable of grasping and basking in the moment of the Transfiguration. Nothing is required of them in that moment other than to simply be. But they want to do something. They want to build three tents (Mark 9:2-10).

Jesus invented servant leadership, but his disciples seemed unable to grasp the concept right up until the end. At the Last Supper when he washes their feet, they are baffled (John 13:1-17).

And then to crown the list we have Thomas doubting the Resurrection (John 20:24-29).

Jesus was never in an intellectual hurry. His intellectual patience with all manner of people throughout his life was unmatched.

Jesus was never in a spiritual hurry. The calm and intentional pace of his ministry demonstrates that Jesus was never in a spiritual hurry.

One of the most endearing examples of this is the story of Zacchaeus. Jesus playfully calls him down from a tree. How long did it take for Zacchaeus to get down from the tree? Jesus invites himself to eat at Zacchaeus' home. How long did it take to get to his home? Thousands of people were pulling at Jesus all the time, and yet, he took the time to minister to one man, demonstrating that he never rushed spiritual encounters (Luke 19:1-10).

His relationship with his disciples is also an example of Jesus' spiritual patience. He didn't push them or rush them to understand. He patiently waited as they made their way toward spiritual maturity. He was never in a hurry to answer their questions or resolve misunderstandings. And he trusted the Holy Spirit would finish what he had begun.

The time he took in quietude to himself, in what the Scriptures describe as lonely places or places set apart, also demonstrates that he was not in a hurry spiritually.

We all know the distraction in prayer on a day when we have much to do. We all know the temptation to cut our prayer short or skip prayer altogether on those days.

Jesus patiently sought spiritual refreshment and communion with God the Father.

Jesus was never in a hurry.

We seem always to be in a hurry by comparison.

These six words should give us pause: Jesus was never in a hurry. Maybe we shouldn't be either. The world may be moving at a ridiculous speed, but that doesn't mean we have to.

BEAUTIFUL INTERRUPTIONS

Jesus made interruptions beautiful. He handled them masterfully. I have never heard anyone mention this profound aspect of Jesus' life, and yet, we have so much to learn from it.

How do you feel when someone interrupts you?

Do you react or do you respond?

Do you handle interruptions with patience and grace, or are you impatient and rude?

You can tell a lot about a person by the way he handles interruptions. There are many signs that a person is flourishing. Joy is a leading indicator. Other signs include empathy, healthy relationships, resilience, contentment, energy, broad satisfaction across multiple areas of life, willingness to serve others, and responding to interruptions graciously and patiently.

Jesus was never in a hurry, and he welcomed interruptions. His unhurried approach to life predisposed him to handling interruptions with compassion and kindness.

Interruptions were beautiful opportunities for Jesus. They were Holy Moments.

Since I began my quest to slow down to the speed of joy what fascinates me most about Jesus' life is the way he handled interruptions. The role interruptions played in his public life is endlessly intriguing.

Jesus' whole public life was made up of interruptions.

Think about that for a moment. Jesus' whole public life was made up of interruptions. The only role that comes close in our society is that of a mother. I often wonder how Meggie gets anything done. Children always need something. How does she get anything done? But then I realize that tending to the children's needs is how she spends her days. What looks like an interruption to others she just sees as part of her day.

And that's how Jesus saw it. He didn't see them as interruptions at all.

Most of the central figures in the Gospels were interruptions. Most of the most powerful stories from the Gospels began as interruptions.

People were constantly trying to interrupt Jesus. The disciples were constantly rebuking people and trying to turn them away. But Jesus overruled his disciples and invited the interruption.

Jesus loved interruptions. He cherished them. Why? He loved people, he cherished people. He didn't see them as interruptions to some more important work he had to do. He didn't see them as interruptions at all. He saw them as people.

"People brought little children to Jesus for him to place his hands on them and pray for them. But the disciples rebuked them. Jesus said, 'Let the children come to me and do not hinder them. For the kingdom of heaven belongs to such as these'" (Matthew 19:13-14).

There was an interesting dynamic between Jesus, his disciples, and those interrupting Jesus. The attitude of the disciples can perhaps best be summarized as: Leave Jesus alone. Our attitude toward people who interrupt us is often a variant of that: Leave me alone.

I get it. The disciples were just trying to protect Jesus. Their intentions were good. Jesus was no doubt being hounded everywhere he went, but over and over throughout the Gospels, Jesus embraces the interruption, and the interruption becomes the lesson. But we still haven't learned the lesson.

Read one of the Gospels through the lens of interruptions and delete everything that happened as a result of an interruption. You won't have much left. Jesus lived a life of interruptions. Beautiful interruptions.

These interruptions began right after he was born with the arrival of the wise men and the shepherds. His public life began with an interruption when Mary made him aware, "They have no more wine" (John 2:3). But to make the larger point, consider the eighth chapter of Matthew which is almost entirely interruptions. "A leper came to him and knelt before him, saying, 'Lord, if you will, you can make me clean'" (Matthew 8:2). "As Jesus entered Capernaum, a centurion came forward to him, beseeching him and saying, 'Lord, my servant is lying paralyzed at home, in terrible distress'" (Matthew 8:5-6). "The boat was being swamped by waves and they went and woke Jesus, saying, 'Save us Lord, we are perishing'" (Matthew 8:25). "When Jesus came to the country of the Gadarenes, two demoniacs met him, coming out of the tombs" (Matthew 8:28).

John's disciples come to him to clarify his teaching on fasting. The scribes and pharisees are constantly trying to entrap him with their questions. The blind cry out to him to have their sight restored. Lepers beg him for mercy. Mothers and fathers bring their sick children to him to be healed. Crowds clamor around him such that he cannot move. A group of men interrupt Jesus teaching in the temple and throw at his feet a woman who had been caught in adultery. He was interrupted by a Samaritan woman as he sat at Jacob's well. A woman who had been bleeding for twelve years interrupted him. His disciples interrupted him when he was praying. And even on his way to the Cross he was interrupted on numerous occasions to be mocked, comforted, and by others who simply wanted to gawk at him.

Jesus' ministry was carried out in the context of interruptions. Holy interruptions. Beautiful interruptions.

Will this insight change the way you respond to interruptions?

Now let's ponder the way most people handle interruptions.

Most people don't like being interrupted. They are concentrating on whatever is before them. They resent being interrupted. Some get irritated, others mildly annoyed, there are those that get disproportionately angry, and some become rageful.

How do you respond to interruptions?

Just as the disciples were constantly trying to brush off anyone who tried to interrupt Jesus we often deal with interruptions in the same way. We have been culturally trained to view them as inconvenient and bothersome.

The world will teach you how to manage interruptions effectively, but that is not our goal. We are trying to learn how to manage interruptions virtuously.

Stay calm and composed. Take a deep breath before reacting and give yourself a chance to respond. Set boundaries.

Jesus set boundaries when he went to a quiet place alone each day. This was not a time to interrupt him.

Responding with grace to interruptions doesn't mean anyone gets to interrupt you anytime. But if you are going to set boundaries, you need to tell people. You can't just set them in your mind. If you are at home and you need thirty minutes to fully engage in a work project, let your family know. It may also help to set a physical boundary like closing your office door.

Prioritize interruptions. Not all interruptions are equal. What seems urgent to the person interrupting you may be able to wait until later or even tomorrow.

Give the person your full attention for a moment so you can assess the urgency of the interruption. Ask yourself: What is the need? Where is the pain?

If you are not going to attend to it now, politely let the person know you will attend to it later. Provide a specific timeframe if that is possible.

Be patient and respond with kindness, even if you cannot grant some-one's request, you can deny them with kindness.

But here is the secret to making interruptions beautiful. It was in the list, but you may have missed it: Take a deep breath before reacting and give yourself a chance to respond.

It is the moment between stimulus and response that determines our success or failure at so many things in life. The stimulus is the interruption. If you react to the stimulus, it will probably be ugly. But if you take a deep breath before reacting to give yourself a chance to respond, it will be beautiful.

The speed of joy when you are interrupted is to pause.

When something happens (stimulus) most people react, because they have too much to do, and their lives are moving too fast. When you are living at the speed of joy, and something happens (stimulus), you are mindful that there is a space between stimulus and response. In that beautiful space you are given the freedom to thoughtfully choose your response.

If you react, you rob yourself of the chance to respond. And your chances of you being at your best if you react are very low. Conversely, your chances of being at your worst if you respond are very low.

Learning to respond rather than react gives us the time to consider the humanity of the situation so that we can respond virtuously with patience and kindness.

The world sees interruptions as inconvenient and bothersome, but what if we have it all wrong? What did Jesus know about interruptions that we have failed to grasp? What if interruptions are beautiful opportunities?

One of the keys to changing the way you perceive interruptions is to eradicate busy from your life. When we are busy or in a hurry, our chances of handling interruptions graciously is close to zero.

The busyness of your life radically impacts the humanity with which you meet interruptions.

If you decide to make this journey and begin to eradicate busy and slow down to the speed of joy, there will come a time when you will wonder how you are doing. *Am I flourishing?* you may ask yourself. *How will I know when I am flourishing?* you may ask yourself.

Interruptions are a good litmus test. When you are flourishing you will begin to handle the interruptions in your life graciously and patiently, with compassion and kindness.

MARGIN: THE MISSING INGREDIENT

When we reduce the busyness of our lives we create margin.

Margin is the difference between load and limit. If a truck is designed and tested to carry ten thousand pounds and you load eight thousand pounds, the load is well within the limits. This is considered a safe working load. The gap between the load and the limit is called margin, and margin, as we will soon discover, is essential to living life at the speed of joy.

Margin removes the need to be in a hurry. Margin allows us to handle interruptions masterfully like Jesus. Margin is what we're still missing.

Load limits represent the safe operational limit under normal conditions. Load that truck with a ten-thousand-pound limit with twelve thousand pounds and you've got a problem. But loading that truck with ten thousand pounds if you are sending it out into a storm is equally dangerous. Remember: Load limits represent the safe operational limit under normal conditions.

We load our lives up with commitments based on optimal conditions. We don't allow for the unexpected, yet the unexpected is inevitable. That's why so many people's lives are breaking, that's why so many lives are crashing. When load limits are exceeded, this is called a breaking load, and breaking loads lead to failure and catastrophic damage.

We are constantly testing the load limits of our lives. We allow no margin, often take on breaking loads, and are therefore flirting with catastrophe every day.

To slow down to the speed of joy we need to build margin into our days. This margin is time to honor the unexpected but important. Because let's face it, the unexpected is inevitable. You may not know what form the unexpected is going to take, but you can be sure each day, week, and month will involve its fair share of unexpected situations and circumstances.

The problem is we overschedule ourselves. We chronically overcommit our time. Research shows 81% of people admit to overcommitting themselves to tasks, activities, and events that they don't have time to fulfill. This leads us to feel overwhelmed and inadequate.

We make this mistake with our time, and we make the same mistake with money. Most people have no margin in their monthly budget. An unexpected expense will then arise, and we say, "I wasn't expecting the washing machine to need repairs this month." Was it truly unexpected? No. The particulars were unexpected, but unexpected expenses arise every month. We may not know exactly what they will be, but we do know that they will arise.

Margin is simply a matter of knowing our limits and making decisions with our limits in mind. We need to learn to build margin into our schedules and our budgets to maintain a healthy gap between our load and our limits.

Living within your limits decreases stress and anxiety, and living within your limits instantly increases your joy. I first learned this lesson from a recovering alcoholic. He worked in the warehouse and led the team who was responsible for shipping every book that was ordered. He always seemed calm and measured. I only ever heard him raise his voice in a safety scenario, and I only saw him get angry once.

His name was Drew and he was a humble man. Never talked much about himself. We worked together for almost ten years before I learned that he had once owned and operated one of the most successful restaurants and bars in the city. But when his alcoholism demolished his life, he sold the restaurant and set about rebuilding his life.

Over the many years, little by little, I got to know him quite well. He shared his story, and it became clear he had lived a difficult life. One of the central narratives of his life was his alcoholism and his recovery journey. But what stood out was that he didn't blame anyone other than himself for what had happened in his life. His sense of personal responsibility was remarkable and admirable.

Drew taught our team so much about life. Some of the lessons I was aware of at the time, but others I didn't come to appreciate until many years after he had moved on to pursue another dream.

He used to share these sayings he heard at his AA meetings. He would inject them into everyday situations with the team.

"One day at a time."
"Keep it simple."
"First things first."
"Cultivate an attitude of gratitude."
"This too shall pass."
"Let go and let God."
"Easy does it."
"Nothing changes if nothing changes."

And he used to talk a lot about the H.A.L.T. rule. H.A.L.T. refers to hungry, angry, lonely, and tired. The idea is that when we get hungry, angry, lonely, and tired we are susceptible to self-destructive behaviors. For an alcoholic that includes relapsing into drinking.

We all know these feelings. They are warnings that our load is approaching our limits.

Learning to recognize the onset of these states (hungry, angry, lonely, and tired) is critical for managing stress, anxiety, addiction, and mood. The H.A.L.T. rule encourages people to check in with themselves regularly to ensure these basic human needs are being met. While they may seem obvious it's amazing how often we overlook these basic needs and common stressors.

This was just one aspect of the most significant lesson Drew taught me. It was about the importance of margin, and the boundaries necessary to protect margin.

It was early one Friday evening when I wandered into the warehouse and found him packing up to go home. The rest of that team had already left, and there were still over a hundred orders to prepare for shipment.

Drew must have read something in the look on my face because he said, "I've been here for twelve hours. It wouldn't be good for me to work any longer today. I'm not scheduled to work tomorrow, but I am planning to come in and finish these orders. I'm happy to do that, but right now I need to go home. I'm getting hungry and tired and that's dangerous territory for me."

I respected that. I respected his clarity and honesty in the moment, and I respect the overarching idea even more today. He knew his load and he knew his limits, and because of his history with alcohol he was careful to guard against getting too close to that line.

The more I got to know Drew the more I discovered the ways he built margin into his life. He did it to stay healthy. He did it to protect against relapsing into alcoholism. He did it to maintain healthy relationships with his wife and children. This margin was nonnegotiable for him.

I have never met anyone who was more aware of his limits and the need for margin. But you don't need to be a recovering alcoholic to adopt the wisdom of margin.

You need margin and boundaries to flourish.

When we have no margin in our days we tend to deal with interruptions very poorly. Lack of margin brings out the worst in people. Margin brings out the best in people. It helps us to flourish.

When we have no margin in our days, we tend to become very focused on ourselves. When we don't have enough time to get everything done, we don't have time for other people.

So, let's connect the dots. We cannot live out the great human mandate to love if we don't have margin. You cannot plan and schedule love. It makes unexpected requests, invitations, and demands of us.

The more we rush around, the less capable we are of loving each other. The more we busy ourselves beyond our limits, the less we are capable of love. Our capacity to love is being diminished by the speed and busyness of our lives. Think about that for a moment. Our capacity to love is being diminished. That is no small thing.

Many of life's finest moments happen in the margin. They are unexpected moments and cannot be scheduled. If we have no margin those moments happen without us. We miss them.

And virtue requires margin. From time to time, you can stretch yourself to be patient and compassionate, courageous and generous. But virtue thrives in the margin. Patience is easier if you have margin. It is easier to be compassionate if you have time to spend with someone who is suffering. Virtue thrives in the margin.

We are desperately in need of some healthy margin in our lives. Establishing healthy margin is essential to human flourishing. We need a reasonable gap between our load and our limits. Margin is crucial to our physical health, our mental health, vibrant relationships, long-term professional satisfaction, and good decision-making.

The wisdom of margin is also necessary to open ourselves to the possibility that interruptions are beautiful. Without this margin we will see every interruption as an annoyance. We need margin so that when life surprises us we can respond gracefully.

I had no margin when I was first trying to slow down to the speed of joy. That's why I kept failing. I didn't realize I was always in a rush until my first attempts to slow down to the speed of joy. I walked fast, ate quickly, rushed through meetings, drove fast, rushed my work, and I was impatient with anything and everyone that slowed me down in any way.

I didn't realize how busy I was either. It was insane. It was like I had five full-time jobs. There wasn't room in my life for any of the good things I needed. I was crowding them out with things that were urgent but not important.

Is there room in your life for the life you want?

Slowing down to the speed of joy will do things for you like: increase your personal and professional satisfaction; prevent stress, anxiety, and burnout; enhance your relationships with family, friends, and colleagues; increase your flexibility and adaptability; teach you to be calm in a crisis; give you the clarity you need to make better decisions; increase your creativity; and expand your capacity to love and be loved.

It will do these things and many more for you, but you need to give it margin to work with.

That's why it's best not to push our commitments to the limits of our capacity. The unexpected is inevitable. We need margin to thrive, so we should reserve some bandwidth for the unexpected. Build margin into your plans so the unexpected doesn't throw your life into disarray.

We create margin by reducing busyness and reducing busyness allows us to slow down to the speed of joy.

It's time to make room in your life for the life you really want. Create margin. Know your limits, live within your limits, and you will flourish.

## PART THREE

THE ONE THING

LIFE ISN'T SUPPOSED TO BE HACKED

A life hack is a technique adopted to simplify an activity. Life hacks are often clever strategies to accomplish tasks more efficiently. Here are some examples: Use different colored nail polish to identify keys. Freeze grapes to chill your drink without watering it down. Put a wooden spoon over a pot of boiling water to keep it from boiling over. Use a cheese grater to quickly soften hard butter. If you're having trouble staying awake in a meeting, or in class, keep one foot slightly off the ground for as long as you can.

There's nothing wrong with life hacks. They are clever. Some of them are brilliant. But why do we need life hacks? Life isn't supposed to be hacked. We shouldn't need to hack life. We should be able to live a deeply fulfilling life without hacking. Something is intrinsically wrong with the idea that life needs to be hacked. Sick and sad. It is evidence that something is profoundly broken.

Life shouldn't need to be hacked.

Why are we in such a hurry anyway? Why are we so busy that we need to do two things at once? And the life hack mentality drives us to do even more even faster. Life hackers think about every possibility in any situation. It is brilliant and creative, but the mind speed required can be exhausting. And it's hard to turn that type of thinking off, or even slow it down, and just be. Why can't we just enjoy doing one thing at a time? Are we capable of doing nothing? The life hack mentality rushes the now. Why can't we be present to the now?

Life is the now.

Slowing down to the speed of joy allows us to fully experience the now. It isn't the breathless thrashing of doing or grasping or seizing or taking—it's about receiving.

Now, let's take another look at two points from earlier.

Jesus was never in a rush. He lived an unhurried life. He was a peaceful presence. He brought a calm to every room he entered. He was present to whoever was before him in that moment. He gave his wholehearted attention to the person he was with in the moment, he gave his whole self to whatever activity he was doing. If he was eating a meal with his disciples, he wasn't preoccupied with the next village they were going to visit. If he was talking to someone, he wasn't looking over their shoulder to see who else was there. He was where he was. And Jesus didn't hustle as fast as he could from one place to the next. He lived at a leisurely pace. He did everything wholeheartedly. He knew how much activity was enough for a single day.

Leisurely means to do something in a relaxed and unhurried way. How often are you able to live at a leisurely pace? What needs to change about your life to make that possible?

Here is the second point.

We find ourselves in a conundrum as modern Christians when it comes to the speed and busyness of our lives. The speed of our lives is unchristian. The busyness of our lives is unchristian. There is no justification for this speed or busyness in the Gospels. Quite the opposite in fact. Urgent, busy, and hurry prevent us from fulfilling the great human mandate to love.

When we're living too fast and our lives are too busy, our hearts become troubled with the things of this world. The speed creates stress and anxiety. The busyness creates stress and anxiety. Both of these lifestyle choices negatively impact our ability to recognize other people's needs and to live out God's mandate to love.

The speed and busyness of our lives are robbing our peace. Jesus bestowed peace on us. "Peace be with you, my peace I give you," were his words (John 14:27). He gave it to us, have we lost it? And how do we recover this peace?

God calls us to a peaceful *way of life*. We will not have peace in our hearts and homes if our *way of life* is chaotic. The speed of joy teaches us how to establish a peaceful *way of life*.

Trying to hack life isn't the answer.

WHO STOLE OUR LEISURE?

We are entering into the heart of this book now. We have a tragically mistaken understanding of leisure and its role in our lives. We think it's about escaping work, but it isn't.

If we don't learn to incorporate leisure into our lives, we will never escape the tyranny of always working. If we don't learn to exist beyond work, we will never embrace leisure, learn to flourish, and live a fully human life. Leisure is that essential.

The question that naturally emerges is: Why do we know so little about something that is so essential to our lives?

What is leisure? Leisure is defined by dictionaries as "free time" and "use of time for enjoyment." But it is so much more than that.

We mistakenly believe that leisure is about not having to work. We think it's time to do nothing, or time to do whatever we want, but it is so much more than that.

Leisure is not merely a break from work so we can get reenergized to go back to work. But consciously or unconsciously, many people believe this is the purpose of leisure. This is the fruit of some of the concepts from our discussion of the history of busy: efficiency, time is money, the rise of the workaholic, and the glorification of busy.

The human efficiency movement grew out of witnessing the efficiency of machines. This gave birth to a desire for people to behave more like machines, but they knew people would reject such blatant dehumanization. So, they called it efficiency, and made us compete with each other to be the best at it. So, it is easy to see how we developed a distorted view of leisure.

Leisure is the opposite of the modern demand for incessant activity. It is the authentic opposite of busy. The busyness of our lives is unleisurely.

Leisure teaches us what is meaningful. Leisure teaches us that you cannot live a meaningful life by filling it with meaningless activity. We say we want to live meaningful lives, but we have severed our relationship with the source of meaning. Leisure repairs that relationship by teaching us which activities are meaningful and how to participate in them.

Leisure expands our capacity to give and receive. It allows us to honestly assess the balance between giving and receiving in our lives, and if we find them out of balance, leisure will help us to rectify that.

Leisure brings us into harmony with ourselves. It allows us to be still and quiet. It gives the truth and goodness of life an opportunity to reveal itself to us. Are you living in harmony with yourself?

The Roman philosopher Seneca observed, "Without leisure, life is not living, it is merely existing." So many people feel Seneca's words every day. They feel like they are merely surviving. Thomas Jefferson wrote, "It is in moments of leisure that we best find ourselves." And how are we to fully live if we have not yet found our truest selves?

When we work too long and too hard, we lose sight of who we are and what we are here for. Leisure reminds us of who we are and what we are here for. Leisure fills us with energy and enthusiasm to return to the world and carry out what we know in our hearts to be our mission in life.

We have cast aside leisure in order to buy more stuff, but I know someone who can help us out of this predicament.

Sometimes in my seminars I ask participants to choose someone, living or dead, to take a road trip with. Other times I ask them if they could invite ten people, living or dead, to dinner in their home, who would they invite?

I would love to take a road trip with Josef Pieper. In 1948, as the world was trying to recover from World War II and everyone was focused on kickstarting their nation's economy, the German philosopher Josef Pieper wrote the short but brilliant work, *Leisure: The Basis of Culture*. It is an epic piece. It is prophetic in many ways. So much of what he feared and warned us against has become normal in our lives and society today.

Pieper provided this richer, more complete definition: "Leisure is an attitude of mind and a condition of the soul that fosters a capacity to receive the reality of the world."

It becomes clear immediately that leisure is a gift. It's something we receive, not something we seize. The crucial question becomes: How do we open ourselves to receive the gifts leisure yearns to lavish upon us?

But first, let's break down Pieper's definition of leisure.

Pieper begins with, "Leisure is an attitude," and later he further explains, "Leisure is not the attitude of the one who intervenes. . .

Not the attitude of someone who seizes," but rather, it is the attitude of "one who opens himself," the attitude "of someone who lets go." Leisure is not about doing, seizing, and conquering—it's about pondering and receiving.

Do we live to work, or do we work to live? This is the central question that drives our approach to leisure. The culture has absorbed distorted notions over hundreds of years, so much so that these false ideas might as well be in the water we drink. They make work primary and encourage us to focus on work. But the great thinkers all the way back to Aristotle encourage us to focus on leisure. Most people have leisure so that they can go back to work refreshed. If this approach is true, then rest exists only so that more work can be accomplished. That would mean our purpose is to work. But Pieper rejects this notion and proposes it is preferable to work so we may pursue something more important—leisure.

True leisure is a condition of the soul, not the absence of work. It isn't doing nothing. It is doing something, but specific types of activity, which allow us to adopt an attitude of inward calm. Leisure teaches us to become a "person who is essentially oriented toward the whole of reality."

Leisure enables us to go out into the world and remain fully human.

Leisure ushers us into harmony with ourselves.

But here's the problem: We are bad at leisure. Either because we don't know what it really is, or because our concept of leisure has been poisoned by our work-obsessed culture, or because we don't know how to do it, or because we are so overwhelmed going to work, raising our children, and paying our bills that we can't possibly imagine stepping away from all that for even a minute.

Whatever the reason, it doesn't matter, because we are going to change all this in a few short pages. Before too long you will know exactly how to participate in one very specific form of leisure, and that one form of leisure will change your life.

It's time to get good at leisure.

Blaise Pascal observed, "All of humanity's problems stem from man's inability to sit quietly in a room." Do you think that's true? Maybe it is and maybe it isn't, but most of us will never know because our ability to sit still in a room is extremely limited. We live lives of constant distraction and perpetual movement. Many people would rather have major dentistry performed than sit quiet and still in a room for an hour.

And perhaps all of humanity's problems are too much to fathom right now, so let's translate Pascal's observation to the individual level. The quote would then read: All of your problems stem from your inability to sit quietly in a room.

Why did he believe sitting in quiet reflection to be so important? Perhaps it was because the time sitting quietly brings us peace and perspective, and these tend to give birth to excellent decisions. If we do not take time to sit still, if we don't take time for quiet reflection, we are much more likely to make poor decisions, foolish decisions that create the problems of our lives.

But sitting still and quiet in your room is not the one very specific form of leisure that will change your life. That is still to come.

THE BASIS OF CULTURE

I wonder what it was like during the days when the Roman Empire was collapsing. Most people were probably just going about their everyday lives. Their entire way of life was about to be obliterated, but they were oblivious to what was happening because they were too busy to notice.

We are witnessing the collapse of Western Civilization, but most people are too busy to notice. Every day we are confronted with more evidence that our culture is in decline. The speed and busyness of our lives is probably evidence enough, but most people give it no thought.

Twenty-five years ago, I wrote these words:

"We are living during a very interesting period of history, a time of transition. Transition periods are the most important, yet you rarely read about them in history books, because it's difficult to judge exactly when they begin and when they end. They lie subtly sandwiched between other periods in history. We are living in such a transition period now.

The reality is that our civilization is in decline. There are five signs that emerge in a declining civilization. These signs can be found in the decline of almost every civilization in recorded history.

The five signs of a declining civilization are:

- *a dramatic increase in sexual promiscuity;*
- *the political undermining and disintegration of family values;*
- *the cultural destruction of the family unit;*
- *the killing of the innocent; and*
- *a radical increase in non-warfare violence.*

These signs have played a major role in the decline and collapse of every civilization in recorded history. So much so that once these signs have emerged to some level of general occurrence and acceptance, no civilization has been able to prolong its existence for longer than one hundred years."

These five signs have been playing out before us for decades. Western civilization is disintegrating before our eyes. We are witnessing the collapse of a culture, and the emergence of a new culture which lacks the truth, beauty, and goodness of the one we seem so willing to discard.

The subtitle of Pieper's work on leisure is: *The Basis of Culture*. It's an enormous claim. Is leisure the basis of culture? It's a bold claim. But if leisure is the basis of culture, and we have abandoned leisure, it should be no surprise that our culture is decaying.

And yet, while the decay and dysfunction of our culture is on full display, we still have the audacity to demand morally responsible leaders who think critically, act wisely, and work tirelessly to advance the common good. This is a reprehensible request because we have destroyed, ridiculed, and expelled everything from society necessary to raise up men and women such as these to lead us.

The Greeks and medieval Europeans understood the tremendous value leisure brought to a culture. "Leisure has been and always will be the first foundation of any culture," Pieper points out. This is why our culture is crumbling. We have destroyed its foundations.

But perhaps the most fascinating point that Pieper makes, given our current circumstances, is that religion can only be born in leisure, a leisure that allows time to contemplate nature, self, God, and the world.

There it is: Religion can only be born in leisure.

Let those who have ears listen: Deprive people of leisure and you will drive religion out of their lives. And isn't that exactly what has happened?

The cover of the original edition of *Leisure: The Basis of Culture* states: "Pieper maintains that our world of total labor has vanquished leisure and issues a startling warning: Unless we regain the art of silence and insight, the ability for non-activity, unless we substitute true leisure for our hectic amusements, we will destroy our culture—and ourselves."

What are your hectic amusements?

How would you rate your friendship with silence?

Leisure dissolves busy. It effortlessly slows our lives to the speed of joy. How important is leisure to our lives and to our society?

Let me repeat myself:

If we don't learn to incorporate leisure into our lives, we will never escape the tyranny of always working. If we don't learn to exist beyond work, we will never embrace leisure, learn to flourish, and live a fully human life. Leisure is that essential.

It is time we returned to an authentic practice of leisure. The fruits of leisure hold the ability to solve so many of our problems, both personally and as a society.

Now let's explore how to create authentic leisure in our lives.

A PROFESSOR'S SABBATICAL

Would you like a year off?

A year off from what?

What would you do?

And why do you desire this time?

Are you tired? Exhausted? Do you just need to rest? Or are you hungry to learn new things?

Think deeper? Pray deeper? Go on an adventure?

A couple of years ago, I ran into a professor from a university on the West Coast. We had worked together on a project many years ago, but I was surprised to see him in Cincinnati. I asked what he was doing in town, and he explained he was on sabbatical.

"Sabbatical. I didn't know they did that anymore?" I exclaimed.

"Yes. It's still very common in academia. I have a full year, but it is more common to have six months now," my professor friend explained.

"Why Cincinnati?" I asked.

"My father grew up here and I wanted to spend some time with him. My mother passed last year and that was an awakening for me."

"A whole year," I said almost involuntarily. "What will you do?"

"I don't have any plans," he said with a smile. I was perplexed and he could tell, so he continued. "Most people make all these plans for their sabbatical. They overload the time with all sorts of activities. And then what they do is they approach their sabbatical just like they would a huge and complex project at work. I made that mistake years ago when I had a three-month sabbatical. I made a twelve-week plan. Every week had activities and outcomes. It was exhausting."

"No plans?" I questioned, still confused about how he was going to use or structure a whole year away from his duties as a professor.

"One plan. Wake up each morning and see what the day has to offer," he said.

"Wow," I exclaimed. "How far into the year are you?"

"About two months."

"What have you been doing?"

"Reading, walking, visiting with my dad and his friends, thinking, praying, resting."

On this day when I bumped into the professor, I had been personally working on slowing down to the speed of joy for three years and found the idea of a sabbatical alluring. But who can take a year off? Even so, the idea of a year off, or even six months, holds great appeal.

Would you like to take a sabbatical for a year? How do you think it would change your life?

The encounter with the professor got me thinking about the idea and I started doing some reading on the subject. I read some fascinating stories.

Oliver traveled around the world in fifty-two weeks. "My sabbatical gave me a fresh perspective on life," he wrote. "It opened my eyes to the world and the diversity of cultures, and renewed my sense of purpose."

Cady found a new way of working, which allowed her to carry the lessons from her sabbatical into everyday life when her sabbatical was over. "My break taught me to tolerate a different way of working, one that isn't filled with daily emergencies and mini-crises. One that includes days off and time to explore creative hobbies and interests."

Sarah and Andrew went sailing. "In a world that often glorifies non-stop productivity, the idea of taking a sabbatical can be met with skepticism. However, I firmly believe that the benefits of a sabbatical far outweigh any potential drawbacks."

The majority of organizations don't offer sabbaticals, so Samantha self-funded hers, saving up over a number of years to make it possible. "My six-month sabbatical shifted my entire outlook on life and will be the gift that keeps on giving—it shifted my entire perspective about how to live life on your own terms."

Ivan took a gap year at thirty-four. "After working more than ten hours per day for eight years, when I suddenly stopped, I realized I had become addicted to being busy—I needed to go through a process of detox to learn how to relax and enjoy my life (outside of work)."

The idea of a sabbatical may seem impossible to you. I get that. But it sure is appealing.

Bill Gates famously takes two weeks each year to think. He calls these "Think Weeks." He takes a break from technology and society in a cabin near Seattle for a week. He began this practice in the '90s. No computer, no phone, and no Wi-Fi. Just lots of books, academic papers, pencils, and Diet Coke.

These Think Weeks had a work focus for Gates, but the work was a very different type of work than leading Microsoft every day.

Michael Karnjanaprakorn, the founder of Skillshare, had this to say about Think Weeks: "I know what you're thinking—who can afford to take a whole week off from work? I look at my Think Weeks as a solution to what I call the 'execution trap.' We stay really busy to keep moving the ball forward on our ideas. But what happens when we move the ball in the wrong direction? The busier you are, the more you can't afford not to take a Think Week."

Does the idea of taking a Think Week appeal to you? How do you think it would change your life?

I spent a week writing in Paris not too long ago. I wrote for six to eight hours twice a day, with a walk and a nap in between. Why Paris? It's an incredible city. Lots of inspiration. Great writers have done great writing there. I'm not sure I really know, but it was amazing. Was that work? Play? Leisure? Learning? A combination of all I suspect. But it was incredibly rewarding. Would you like a week in Paris? What would you do? How would it change your life?

There is something about these stories that stirs something deep within us. Whatever that is I think we should start paying more attention to it. A sabbatical, a Think Week, retreats, pilgrimages, a day of recollection, a reading day, a day of prayer—there are so many ways to access the fruits of the sabbatical spirit. We may think these things are impossible, but in the next chapter I will share with you how we can all do these things.

THE ONE THING

Sunday.

That's the one thing. That's what you're yearning for. And it will change your life in ways you cannot even begin to imagine.

Sabbath.

That's what is stirring deep within you when you hear people's sabbatical stories. The stirring deep within you desires Sabbath. Not a year of rest to catch up on all the rest you missed out on. A day of rest every week. Not Sunday like we've been doing Sunday. A new approach. It's time to reimagine our experience of Sundays.

Resist it. Doubt it. Ignore it. Avoid it. But Sabbath is the one thing. Ever ancient and ever new.

The uncomfortable truth is that God gives us a mini-sabbatical every week. Have you been surrendering to the joy God wants to give you through the genius of the Sabbath? I know I have squandered my fair share.

Sunday is the one thing. I promised you one very specific form of leisure that will change your life. Sunday is it. The wisdom of the Sabbath will teach you how to slow down to the speed of joy. It's the one thing that will help you to restore your capacity for leisure and lead you to flourish like never before. Sunday will create margin to love like never before and carry out the great human mandate to love God and neighbor wholeheartedly. Sunday is the one thing from which so many other good things will flow. Goodness you cannot imagine yet will flow from authentically embracing Sundays.

That's the one thing. The world is full of lists. It would have been so easy to write you a list of twelve ways to slow down to the speed of joy, but that would have given you eleven reasons not to take seriously the one that will make all the difference.

Lists are fun. People love lists. The most popular videos on my YouTube channel are lists:

24 Regrets of People Who Are Dying

4 Toxic Everyday Habits That Are Killing You

9 Ways to Tell If Someone Is a Narcissist

10 Things You Should Never Say to Anyone

Lists are easy to write and easy to ignore. Sometimes what we need is the genius of simplicity, the piercing clarity of the one thing. So that's what I decided to give you. Here is the Russian Proverb appropriate to our situation: "If you chase two rabbits, you will catch neither."

Sunday is the answer. It's our rabbit. It's the one thing.

We are often tempted to reject the simple. "It couldn't be that simple," we tell ourselves. But it is. Think about it like this: Have you ever tried it? Have you ever really set Sundays as a day of rest?

Try it. Test it. Prove it to yourself one way or another. Set Sunday aside in the way we are about to discuss for one month. After just four Sundays, I think you will find that you see yourself differently, you're more engaged in relationships, the other people in your life love being with you on Sundays, you have a healthier perspective of what matters most in life, and you will be beginning to flourish.

It's time to do Sunday different.

Sunday is your mini-sabbatical. It's a think day, a read day, a pray day, a time of leisure, a chance to flourish, a fountain of joy, and a day of rest.

Do you need a day of rest?

I know I do. Often. Regularly. I see all the craziness of our lives, rushing here and there, the endless busyness, and I hear a faint voice in the distance. It is Jesus. He is beckoning to us, "Come to me all you who are weary and heavy burdened I will give you rest" (Matthew 11:28).

Are you weary? Are your burdens heavy?

The creation story in Genesis depicts God creating the light and the waters, the trees and the plants, the day and the night, the sea and the air, all the animals, and the man and the woman. At the end of each day, God reflected on his work that day and concluded, "It was good."

God set the seventh day aside for rest, "and He rested on the seventh day" (Genesis 2:2). Why? I'm not being facetious. Why did God rest on the seventh day? He didn't need to rest. God is an infinite being. He has no need for rest. So, why did God rest? He rested because he knew we would need to rest.

We have a legitimate need for rest. That's why God built it into the lifestyle he imagined for us.

The Hebrew word "Shabbat" from which we draw the English word "Sabbath" means "to stop." It's a day to stop. What do we need to stop? Working, complaining, hurrying, worrying, wanting, obsessing over our phone, chasing, listening to the negativity of so much modern content, taking everything personally, and we need to stop ignoring signs. Engage your mystical sense. Open yourself to divine guidance. Listen to your heart. Really listen.

Sabbath is the ultimate form of margin, not to do all the stuff you didn't get done during the week, but to engage and refresh the body, heart, mind, and soul with leisure.

It's interesting that the lifestyle images used to sell us vacations and retirement plans often portray Sabbath lifestyle. They are full of time alone with family and friends and carefree timelessness. Advertisements for all manner of products and experiences depict people slowing down to the speed of joy. They are at leisure. They are unhurried. They are joyful. Even Madison Avenue marketers remember what most of us have forgotten: We all yearn for what the Sabbath desires to give us freely. Meanwhile corporations are trying to sell us things that cannot deliver what they promise.

We need to *Shabbat*. We need to stop.

You may be asking, "Why do we need to stop? I thought we were slowing down to the speed of joy." We are. But in order to find the speed of joy, we need to slow down, we need to pause, we need to stop.

Let me explain. It has to do with speed distortion. If you are driving at 100 mph along a highway and you slow down to 80 mph, you will feel like you are crawling at a snail's pace. You will feel like you are going painfully slow. This is speed distortion.

Take the same example, but this time, instead of slowing down from 100 mph, you stop to get a coffee and some gas. When you resume your journey, you drive at 80 mph. You don't experience speed distortion in the same way. Stopping is the only way to deal with speed distortion. We need Shabbat. We need to stop. Sunday is a perfect opportunity.

I know. You have too much to do. I know because I still end up in that mindset some Sundays. I'm disappointed in myself, but it's the truth. Here's the sad part: When I honor the Sabbath, I get more done in six days than I could in seven days. Honoring the Sabbath brings clarity that allows you to focus on the right things. Resting on Sundays allows you to return to your work with renewed energy and enthusiasm.

Observing Sunday as a day of rest liberates us from those feelings of hurried, overwhelmed, and anxious. Doing Sunday right makes the other six days better. It makes the other six days more focused and meaningful. I get more done because I am focused on the right things. I have more energy and enthusiasm for every aspect of my life.

The Sabbath is more than a day of rest. It is a day of rejuvenation, realignment, and renewal. It's a day to set aside everything that seems urgent so we can be reminded of what is important.

Sabbath reminds us that the most important things are hardly ever urgent. When did you last need to urgently exercise? When was the last time you urgently needed to spend a few hours connecting with your spouse? Have you ever urgently needed to read a great book? Do you ever need to urgently eat a healthy meal? When did you last urgently need to spend an hour in prayer?

The Sabbath is an invitation to fall in love again.

Have you ever wondered how young people fall in love so easily and the rest of us fall out of love so easily? Carefree timelessness. What's that? Carefree timelessness is time together without an agenda.

Teenagers are experts at it. They go out with friends for hours and you ask, "What did you do?" "Nothing," they say. They spend hours texting or talking and you ask, "What did you talk about?" They reply, "Nothing." You think they are being evasive or dismissive, but they may just be telling the truth. And our adult relationships could benefit tremendously from some of the same nothing.

Carefree timelessness is the reason young people fall in love so easily, and lack of carefree timelessness is the reason the rest of us fall out of love so easily.

You had plenty of carefree timelessness when you were falling in love. You made it a priority.

All relationships thrive if you give them carefree timelessness, but we don't. We try to shove them into five minutes here and ten minutes there. Do we actually believe relationships can thrive under these conditions? Do we sincerely feel that this is enough to form a significant connection with another human being? Or have we simply failed to think about it because we are distracted by the everyday insanity of our busy lives?

The Sabbath is an invitation to fall in love again—with life, with God, with each other.

Sundays are beautiful. When was the last time you really experienced Sabbath? How long has it been since you tasted the joy of the Sabbath? Think about it. The joy of the Sabbath. It may have been a while. It may have been a very long while.

But it's on quiet Sunday afternoons that we will discover what Rilke and Kafka were on about.

"You do not need to leave your room. Remain sitting at your table and listen. Do not even listen, simply wait, be quiet, still and solitary. The world will freely offer itself to you to be unmasked, it has no choice, it will roll in ecstasy at your feet." —Franz Kafka

"Be patient toward all that is unsolved in your heart and try to love the questions themselves, like locked rooms and like books that are now written in a very foreign tongue. Do not now seek the answers, which cannot be given you because you would not be able to live them. And the point is, to live everything. Live the questions now. Perhaps you will then gradually, without noticing it, live along some distant day into the answer." —Rainer Maria Rilke

Open yourself to a deep experience of the Sabbath and the answers to questions you have long sought will effortlessly appear in your heart.

The Sabbath is a giver of gifts. Whatever good things you want to increase in your life, honor the Sabbath and it shall be so. This is the secret power of the Sabbath. I cannot explain it fully. But reflect upon what it is you most want to increase in your life: Do you want a relationship to improve? Do you want to become healthier? Do you want more success in your career? Do you want to be a better parent? Do you want less stress and anxiety? Do you want the quality of your friendships to improve? Do you want to become a better decision maker?

Whatever it is, whatever good things you desire to fill your life, honor the Sabbath and it will be so.

But there is a gift the Sabbath will give you that is beyond compare. If you faithfully observe this holy day, like Abraham, you will become a friend of God (James 2:23). You will learn to see the hand of God at work in your life. You will learn to discern the slightest nudge that God gives you in one direction or another. The Spirit of God will be upon you. God will whisper to you through the Scriptures and as you go about your day, you will delight in his voice. Like the morning sun you will feel the warmth of his smile upon your face, and you will rejoice in the new life he has given you.

All you have to do is surrender to the Sabbath.

WHAT HAPPENED TO SUNDAY?

At the 1924 Olympics, the 100-meter race was set to be a showdown for the ages between the English runner Harold Abrahams, the American Charley Paddock who had won the gold medal at the 1920 Olympics, and Eric Liddell, a Scottish rugby player and sprinter. But the epic clash was not to be.

Eric Liddell was a committed Christian and refused to run on Sundays in observance of the Sabbath. Pressure was put on him to run by just about every authority that had any influence on him. But he stood his ground.

Harold Abrahams went on to win the 100-meter dash. Eric Liddell changed events to the 400-meter dash in order to compete. He won the gold medal and set a world record. And this is what he said, "I believe God made me for a purpose, but he also made me fast. And when I run, I feel His pleasure." When was the last time you felt God's pleasure?

But that was a different time. One hundred years ago. When I was a child all the stores were closed on Sundays. You couldn't buy anything on a Sunday. And we never played sports on Sundays. But that was a different time. Forty years ago.

Times may have changed, but God's dreams for his children have not. If we think we are going to find happiness by disregarding God's schedule we have lost touch with reality in exactly the ways Pieper predicted.

What happened to Sunday?

Did you know it was once illegal to disturb the Sabbath in the United States? Here is an excerpt from *A Bill for Punishing Disturbers of Religious Worship and Sabbath Breakers*, June 18, 1779: "If any person on Sunday shall himself be found laboring at his own or any other trade or calling, or shall employ his apprentices, servants or slaves in labor, or other business, except it be in the ordinary household offices of daily necessity, or other work of necessity or charity, he shall forfeit the sum of ten shillings for every such offence, deeming every apprentice, servant, or slave so employed, and every day he shall be so employed as constituting a distinct offence."

At one point the Sabbath—your Sabbath, my Sabbath, our Sabbath—was clearly defended and preserved. What happened? Who stole the Sabbath?

The sad thing is we stole it from ourselves. It might be more accurate to say we traded it away. We made a bad deal and now we are living with the bad deal. We traded our Sundays away for more money, more stuff, and more convenience. That's the short answer. And we lost more than a day of rest. It disrupted the rhythm of life, knocked us out of harmony with ourselves, and left us confused and anxious.

It was a bad deal. Now it's time to renegotiate.

# # #

I know. You think you can't do it. But you can. Let's talk about how. Discovering that you can do something that you thought you couldn't instills confidence, and provides a blueprint for the next time you think something isn't possible.

Don't let what you can't do interfere with what you can do. This is the first rule when it comes to impossible thinking.

Next, identify your immovable obstacles. For example, someone might say, "I can't take back my Sundays and take the Sabbath as a day of rest because my shift at work starts on Sunday night at 6 p.m." No problem. We have identified your immoveable obstacle. You may not be able to change your shift immediately, but it may become possible now that you know it's important to you.

"I can't take back my Sundays because I volunteer to babysit so young couples can go to church," another person may say. No problem. We may have identified your immoveable obstacle.

"My daughter has a soccer match every Sunday at noon," another person might say. Not ideal. But this is the world we live in today. We know your immoveable obstacle.

Whatever the immovable obstacle is, keep one thing in mind. Most immoveable obstacles are only immovable in the short-term. It's also important that we don't misidentify an activity. For example, taking care of infants so their parents can go to church may be a form of leisure. It may not seem like leisure at times when they are crying, but it could be a soul-nourishing activity.

Now what we do is we explore all the options, and there are always more options than we think there are when we are stuck in impossible thinking.

I have a friend who has a very demanding job as the CEO of a large corporation. He needs to work Sunday night to set his week up for success. So, he honors the Sabbath from sundown on Saturday night until sundown on Sunday night. One of his friends honors the Sabbath from 6 p.m. on Saturday night until 6 p.m. on Sunday night. They got this idea, of course, from our spiritual ancestors. The Jewish people observe their Shabbat from sundown on Friday to sundown on Saturday.

Design some version of Sabbath for yourself and begin next Sunday. Start small if you must. Focus on what's possible for you right now. It may be just four hours on a Sunday. Great. Celebrate that. Honor that every week. And build from there. The fruits will encourage you to increase four hours to six, and six hours to eight over time.

It may require an epic wrestle. You may have to fight to win every hour of your Sabbath back. It will be worth it and you will treasure every hour of every Sabbath all the more.

Don't let what you can't do interfere with what you can do. Slow down and embrace the life-giving joy every Sunday wants to freely give you.

What happened to Sunday? A few years from now when someone asks this question you will have a great story to tell about how you took back your own Sundays.

PRACTICING THE SABBATH

The calm, purpose, and joy of the Sabbath is an invitation and a lesson. It's an invitation to experience calm, purpose, and joy. And the lesson is that when we live Sabbath well, we learn that all of life can be lived calmly, purposefully, and joyfully.

Rabbi Abraham Joshua Heschel observed, "To observe the Sabbath is to celebrate the infinite worth of time rather than the efficiency of work," and "The Sabbath is not for the sake of the weekdays; the weekdays are for the sake of Sabbath. It is not an interlude but the climax of living."

The fruits of the Sabbath are vast and undeniable, but the Sabbath is not as easy to practice as you might think, and the reasons may surprise you.

The idea of a mini-sabbatical each week has its allure, no doubt, but that is heavily influenced by the burden of our lives under the tyranny of urgent, busy, and hurry.

The biggest challenge to honoring the Sabbath is what surprises many: Work is easier than leisure. That's right. It's much easier to work more than to slow down and learn how to practice Sabbath. One reason is because we know how to work—it is comfortable—whereas we need to learn how to practice Sabbath.

It is easier to work more than to practice true leisure. This is the primary reason people don't spend more time at leisure. Keep that in mind when you feel the pull of busy on Sunday. When you feel drawn to work on Sunday, observe yourself. Is there a real need or are you running away from acquiring the discipline of practicing leisure?

Leisure will become easier over time. But this I promise you: The day will come when there will be nothing you would rather do. Leisure will become a source of euphoria and ecstasy. But it is a difficult habit to acquire in the beginning. I tell you that not to scare you, but to prepare you. The mistaken belief that leisure should be easy is an enemy to success.

Leisure requires two specific disciplines and two specific virtues.

The first discipline leisure requires is one that we are unaccustomed to because we live immersed in a culture addicted to activity. Leisure requires that we learn to do nothing, and most people are horrible at doing nothing.

The second discipline leisure requires we are also unaccustomed to because our culture worships measurable results. Leisure requires that we learn to enjoy doing things just for the joy of it and not because of the outcome it may produce. Just for the joy of it.

Humility and patience are the two specific virtues leisure requires of us. Humility to let go, surrender, and receive. Patience to learn to appreciate simplicity, to practice activities that are not productivity-focused, and to cultivate inner peace and outer calm.

There are many different types of doing nothing from the perspective of leisure. Sitting in silence. Fasting from technology. Reflecting on nature. Doing something just for the joy of it, something that has no utilitarian value. This requires that we let go of the outcomes-based thinking that can be very useful in our professional work but will destroy our chances of fully experiencing leisure. Sitting still. Cloud watching. Listening to the rain.

If you would like to understand just how difficult it is to learn to practice leisure, close your eyes and sit still, completely still, for five minutes.

Doing nothing is the hardest thing in the world. It is also the solution to so many of our problems. How many problems would be avoided if we would learn to hold our tongues? Our bias toward activity leads us to believe that problems can only be solved by doing something. That's false. Our bias toward activity also encourages a belief that success is always the result of doing something. But there are many instances when success is the result of doing nothing.

This is disturbingly true in the case of investing in the stock market. 85% of money managers do not beat the market. That means if you bought an index fund you would beat 85% of money managers. Why? They lack the discipline to do nothing. They react to short-term market fluctuations by trading, rather than investing in quality companies that will produce solid long-term returns. They lack the patience and discipline that has proven to produce the best results in the industry for more than one hundred years.

Sometimes it's not what you do, it's what you don't do, that makes all the difference. This is absolutely true in the case of leisure and the Sabbath. Doing nothing is the hardest thing in the world to do.

The wisdom of the Sabbath is learning to engage in wonderful forms of nothing. The purpose of leisure is to attempt to be purposeless, and when this is achieved, nothing is more purposeful. Or in the timeless wisdom of Winnie-the-Pooh, "Sometimes doing nothing can lead to the very best of something."

LEISURE REVISITED

Learn to do nothing. This is a tough one for me. I have spent my whole life trying to squeeze the most out of each day, each hour, each moment. But this obsession with efficiency often lures me away from what matters most.

Josef Pieper's *Leisure: The Basis of Culture* is a philosophical text but its application to our lives seventy-five years after it was written is astounding.

What is leisure? Pieper provides the answer. "Leisure is an attitude of mind and a condition of the soul that fosters a capacity to receive the reality of the world."

"Capacity to receive the reality of the world." Wow. How often do we turn away from the reality of a situation because it is too much? We can't handle it. How often do we meet people who are in complete denial of reality in some aspect of their life?

The enemies of leisure are what Pieper calls lives of distraction and "total work." Total work and constant distractions both prevent the deep reflection that leisure seeks to lead us into.

Leisure allows us to receive the gifts of wisdom. It teaches us that there is no amount of human effort that can attain this wisdom by itself. Leisure is indispensable in our quest to thrive as human beings in this life and the next.

Why does leisure matter?

Pieper points out that religion can only be authentically born in a person and society through leisure. It cannot be rushed. Leisure is indispensable for the contemplation of God. Leisure is the foundation of culture.

Think on that for a moment: Religion can only be authentically born in a person and society through leisure.

When we discuss why religion has been abandoned by so many people in our culture, and why Western societies have rejected religion at an alarming rate over the past seventy-five years, the reasons we discuss are primarily based in enlightenment academics. These can be summarized by saying that we are no longer in the Dark Ages and people don't need to cling to the superstition of religion. But what Pieper suggests deserves serious consideration.

Is it possible that religion has disappeared from our lives and society because it simply cannot survive without leisure? Leisure is the oxygen that keeps religion alive. And what are the implications of this when it comes to passing faith from one generation to another in societies full of people who are less interested in participating in authentic leisure?

One of the ways Communism seeks to murder religion is through "total work." Total work transforms human beings into workers and nothing more.

The totalitarianism of Communism is a dictatorship and requires complete subservience to the state. Total work is a form of totalitarianism where complete subservience to work is required. Total work is a condition in society that establishes work as the dominant focus of human life, work as people's source of identity, and it is work that consumes every aspect of life.

Total work makes wisdom, culture, religion, and contemplating God impossible. This is why total work was so central to Communism in the twentieth century. In our own place and time, we are imposing the condition of total work upon ourselves.

Even when we're not doing paid work, we busy ourselves with all manner of unpaid work that keeps us from the leisure that is essential to our human flourishing.

"Be still and know that I am God," is the counsel of Psalm 46:10. Pieper translates it as, "Have leisure and know that I am God." But we seem incapable of this stillness and leisure.

Have leisure and know God.

Have leisure and grow in wisdom.

Have leisure and grow to love more deeply.

Have leisure and see the reality of the world as it really is.

Josef Pieper was a great philosopher. He was also a prophet. His work on leisure issued this stark warning, "Total labor vanquishes leisure. Unless we regain the art of silence and insight, the ability for nonactivity, unless we substitute true leisure for our hectic amusements, we will destroy our culture—and ourselves."

Paid and unpaid work of every type—the sheer busyness of our lives—has gobbled up more and more of our time since Pieper penned these words. We have also multiplied our hectic amusements. The result has been exactly as Pieper foresaw.

We have banished silence from our lives. We have replaced wisdom and insight with knowledge and mere information. Our amusements have only become more hectic, and we have been seduced by endless distractions. We have abandoned religion and dismantled culture, we are destroying Western Civilization and, in the process, destroying our very selves.

The hardest thing in the world to do is nothing. Leisure. Reflection. Basking in God's presence. We need to learn to relax. Learn to do nothing. Establish leisure as part of your daily routine. And naturally, when we begin to embrace doing nothing, we realize that leisure, true leisure, is anything but nothing.

It's time to refuse the madness of constantly rushing around doing things that don't matter. It's time to figure out what does matter. It's time to embrace authentic leisure.

Next Sunday would be a great time to start.

LEISURE IS ESSENTIAL TO THE HUMAN EXPERIENCE

Leisure is essential to the human experience. We cannot be fully human without leisure. It profoundly impacts our physical and mental health, our spiritual well-being, and our capacity to love and be loved. Every aspect of our lives improves when we make leisure a habit.

So let's discuss some practical examples. For Pieper, leisure was a form of contemplation marked by an openness to the goodness of the world that increases our ability to perceive reality and our knowledge of what is real. Lots of words there, but let's break it down to some key concepts.

Contemplation: to look at something thoughtfully for an extended period of time. This alone indicates that leisure isn't something to be rushed or done quickly.

Openness: a lack of restriction that affirms accessibility. So much of what we experience can lead us to close and harden our hearts, but an open heart is essential to leisure.

Openness to the goodness of the world: Pieper's belief in the world's goodness was influenced by Aristotle, Plato, Aquinas, and the assertion of the Christian faith that the world is fundamentally good because it was created by God.

Our ability to perceive reality: Contemplation and openness to goodness increase our ability to perceive reality. Many of the false beliefs that permeate the culture close us off from reality. The happiness we experience is limited by the truth and reality of our lives.

Knowledge of what is real: Knowing what is real is central to living a meaningful, deeply fulfilling, and truthful life. Our current culture's unwillingness to differentiate between what is true and false, right and wrong, good and evil, makes it increasingly impossible for people to live happy, meaningful, and deeply satisfying lives.

The busyness of our lives is in direct opposition to leisure. I have referred to "our insanely busy lives" and "the insanity of our busy lives." Insanity is a denial of reality, an inability to distinguish what is real from what is imagined. While leisure increases our ability to perceive reality, the busyness of our lives is in many ways a denial of reality. It denies our limits. We often use it to avoid the reality of uncomfortable situations or distract from the reality of life's most important questions. And busyness denies the reality of our humanity.

The startling discovery is that the relentless busyness of our lives is at odds with reality itself, so it's little wonder that so many people are so desperately unhappy. Severed from reality, how can anyone be happy?

But Pieper offers a road back. Leisure. Authentic leisure. Not just a break from work so we can go back to work to work harder than ever.

The examples of leisure that Pieper celebrated and practiced himself were contemplation, philosophical reflection, celebration, worship, the arts and aesthetic appreciation, true rest, play, and the pursuit of wisdom and knowledge.

Many of these may seem foreign to us at first glance, but if we consider specific examples from each of the categories mentioned above, we will learn they are more familiar to us than we first suspected.

Contemplation and Philosophical Reflection

For Pieper, contemplation and philosophical reflection were forms of leisure that involved quiet reflection on life, nature, existence, and the divine. Sitting quietly in a rocking chair or by the beach, observing the beauty of nature, or thinking about life without a practical goal or specific agenda is an act of leisure.

Celebration and Worship

For Pieper, the highest form of leisure was religious worship and the ultimate good in life was union with God. These acts allow us as human beings to step out of the realm of everyday life, to set aside the responsibilities and concerns of this life, and to enter the realm of the sacred. Celebrations are also a form of leisure as they are opportunities to express gratitude for life, gratitude for each other, and gratitude to God for all the ways he enriches our experience in this world.

The Arts and Aesthetic Appreciation

When we engage with music, paintings, photographs, sculpture, and literature, we have the possibility of experiencing truth, beauty, and goodness without any practical outcome or the expectation of production. Reading a novel, listening to a symphony, visiting a museum, or listening to an album from start to finish are examples of leisure.

True Rest

There is a difference between rest to recover from work and true rest. True rest is made up of a peaceful stillness and an opportunity to exist free from the demands of productivity. The only goals of true rest are to be at peace and engaged meaningfully in the present moment. This could simply mean sitting in a garden and reading a book.

Play

Games and playful activities that have no material goals. Participated in for their own sake, to foster relationship and community, and engaged in for enjoyment and free from the pressure of winning. Hobbies often allow adults to experience this type of leisure, returning us to the wonder and joy of childhood.

Pursuit of Wisdom and Knowledge

Education in modern society is increasingly aimed at the acquisition of marketable skills that can be used to work and earn a living. The pursuit of wisdom and knowledge that we consider a true form of leisure seeks wisdom and knowledge for their own sake. We can participate in this type of leisure through philosophical discussions, reading the classics, or reflecting on life's biggest questions. The joy born from marveling at wisdom is unmatched.

# # #

Meanwhile, America's favorite leisure activity is shopping, which is not leisure at all. It is just another aspect of our obsession with activity and our ongoing slavery to trinkets.

Leisure allows us to rise above the grind of our everyday lives by liberating us from production or outcomes. This naturally elevates us toward things that are more meaningful and opens us to the transcendent and the sacred—around us and within us.

SUNDAY BY DESIGN

"I loaf and invite my soul," wrote Walt Whitman. He understood the hidden power of leisure. He referred to it as loafing. Loafing, as Whitman calls it, opens the heart and mind, and allows peace and tranquility to flow in. We all need time to relax, a time to be quiet and listen. If we will listen to each other, to God, and to the gentle voice within, our lives will be much more peaceful.

"I don't get any peace," I overheard a woman saying to her husband and adult children. It's true for many people I suspect. That's a hard life. Inner peace makes the difficulties of life easier. Inner peace allows us to be at peace with disagreeable people. Inner peace is a treasure that cannot be taken from you. Inner peace isn't the absence of tension or problems or difficulties, it's the belief that in the fullness of time they will all work themselves out.

Leisure is a mighty source of peace.

Leisure increases the richness of life. The wise make time to loaf. But we seem obsessed with speed and activity. We are always busy, everything seems urgent, and we are always hurrying from one thing to the next.

Leonardo da Vinci was born in Italy in 1452. He was a painter, sculptor, architect, musician, engineer, mathematician, and scientist. Da Vinci was unquestionably one of the greatest intellects in human history. This was his advice:

"Every now and then go away,

have a little relaxation,

for when you come back to your work

your judgment will be surer;

since to remain constantly at work

will cause you to lose power of judgment. . .

Go some distance away

because the work appears smaller and

more of it can be taken in at a glance,

and a lack of harmony or proportion

is more readily seen."

When it comes to designing your Sunday experience, I am not going to give you a list of dos and don'ts. But I am going to give two brief thoughts to consider.

You will want to get the most out of your mini-sabbaticals, and that's the first mistake. This is the way we approach almost everything in our lives. It comes from the cult of efficiency. Our life outside of work shouldn't be approached the same way we approach work.

A couple asked for my thoughts on an itinerary for a trip to Paris they were planning. This was my feedback: Do one third of what you are planning to do, and you will have a much better trip. They probably thought I was crazy. I appreciate that it may be the only time they ever visit Paris, but it is better to do a few things well. It is better to experience the City of Lights (or any city for that matter) at the speed of joy, rather than rushing from one thing to another so you can say you did all the things.

We are pilgrims, not tourists. These mini-sabbaticals will not be leisurely and restful if you try to cram too much into them. So, my first piece of advice is do not try to get the most out of each Sunday. Allow the signs and wonders God sends you each Sunday to sink deep into your heart.

The same holds true if you get the chance to take a sabbatical someday. Don't try to do too much. Don't cram too much into your sabbatical plans. Your capacity is far, far less than you think. We are always overestimating what can actually be done in one day. That's how we end up trapped in the endless cycle of urgent, busy, and hurry.

We think we can do more than we can, and we make commitments based on those false estimations. When we're unable to fulfill all these commitments we feel bad about ourselves. One of these feelings is a sense of failure.

When you are practicing leisure, if you ever feel like you are failing, one of two things is wrong. Either your concept of leisure is mistaken or the way you are approaching leisure is flawed. Leisure should never leave you feeling like a failure.

Whether it's any given Sunday, a retreat, a pilgrimage, a Think Week, or a sabbatical—you will get the most out of these experiences by planning the least.

I promised you two brief thoughts. Here's the second. Learn to say no. First, learn to say no to yourself. If you say yes to yourself all the time, sooner or later, your life will be miserable. And learn to say no to other people. You don't have to accept every invitation you receive. Three weeks from now, will anybody know or care if you weren't there?

Say no ruthlessly to everything that isn't leisurely when leisure is your aim. Protect your leisure ruthlessly. Doing too much will stop you from becoming the-best-version-of-yourself. Busy will destroy you. Guard against it fiercely.

THE SIMPLE ART OF TAKING BACK YOUR LIFE

Every book makes a promise. Some authors keep the promise they make to readers, and some don't. It's a burden for an author, but it's also a blessing. The burden is it requires intentionality. The blessing comes in the deep calm that descends when you have finished the final manuscript. You are vulnerable, but at peace. You have opened yourself to others, friends and strangers, and they will accept you or judge you as they see fit, but your part in it is finished.

In that moment, I set the pile of pages on my desk, and sit with them. I pet them like a puppy dog and ponder the question: Have I fulfilled the promise I made to the reader? And in that same moment, I know without a doubt whether I have or haven't. If I haven't, I write another draft.

The Simple Art of Taking Back Your Life is the subtitle of this volume. Can something so significant, something that seems so difficult and complex, be simple? Let's find out.

Our lives have been abducted. The incessant speed of our lives isn't healthy. You know it, I know it, everyone knows it. The ever-increasing busyness of our lives is insane. Everyone knows it. It's time to eliminate urgent, busy, and hurry from our everyday lives. It's time to slow down to the speed of joy. It's time to take back our lives.

How? One Sunday at a time. Take back your life by taking back Sunday. Take back your life one Sunday at a time. Simple? Yes. Easy? No.

The simple art of taking back your life has just one step: Take back your Sundays. But that one step will set off a domino effect that you are simply incapable of imagining right now. Allow me to provide a glimpse:

You will get good at setting boundaries. You will get great at saying no. You will avoid all unnecessary commitments. You will get very clear about what truly matters to you. You will know your values. You will prioritize what matters. You will stop pretending. You will speak your mind with kindness. You'll stop caring what other people think about you. You'll gladly unplug from technology. You will discover how to relax, really relax. You will stop seeing leisure as an unobtainable luxury. The low-grade anxiety everybody experiences in our society will dissipate. You will listen deeply to yourself and others. You will declutter your space, your schedule, and your heart. You will let go of material possessions that don't serve a need or bring you joy. You will be in awe of your productivity when you are working. You will notice yourself breathing and rejoice in it. You will savor food and moments. You will delight in being able to help someone in need because you built margin into your schedule. You will rediscover your spontaneity. Your relationships will be more meaningful than ever. The people you love will feel a profound connection with you, and you will feel profoundly connected to them.

And people will ask you if you are dying, because that's the only time in our insanely busy culture that people live deliberately—when they are dying.

But I've said it before and I will say it again: don't take my word for it. I don't want you to take my word for it. I want you to try it for yourself. Begin this Sunday.

It may be simple, but it won't be easy, and make no mistake, this is a radical, countercultural, revolutionary act. Just as Eric Liddell announcing to the Olympic Committee that he would not run on a Sunday was a radical, countercultural revolutionary act.

Revolutions have a way of building toward a culminating moment. Your personal revolution has probably been building for quite some time. It is my hope that this book has provided the culminating moment.

The buildup to the American Revolution included the Stamp Act (1765), the Boston Massacre (1770), the Boston Tea Party (1773), the First Continental Congress (1774), and the Battles of Lexington and Concord (1775). But on July 4, 1776, with the Declaration of Independence, the colonies declared themselves independent from Britain.

All revolutions have a moment when they begin. This is your moment. Start your personal revolution to take back your life right now. It's time for you to declare your independence from the insane speed and busyness of life that characterizes our age. Set yourself free from the shackles of urgent, busy, and hurry.

Take back your life one Sunday at a time.

You get so few.

My nephew James was born last week. He has about 4,160 Sundays.

4,160. That's how many Sundays most people get. And we waste them. We waste them being too busy. We waste them being hungover. We waste them being unintentional. We waste them letting the culture push us around. We waste them being selfish. We waste our Sundays, and Sundays are too precious to be wasted.

I began this book talking about the thing I would change. The opening lines were. . .

There are people who say they have no regrets. I'm not one of them. If I could go back and live my life all over again there are things I would change. One thing I would change is the speed at which I have lived my life. I would slow my life down, and not just a little.

If I could go back and do it all over again, I'd also change my approach to Sundays. Radically. I wouldn't just tweak my approach, I'd overhaul it. When I look back on the Sundays of my life I have a sense of loss. I squandered so many Sundays.

I have 1,456 left.

If you're twenty years old, you have 3,120.

If you're forty, you have 2,080.

If you're sixty, you have 1,040.

They go fast.

It's time to start taking back your life—one Sunday at a time.

PART FOUR

THE SECRET

OF LIFE

THE SECRET OF LIFE

Humanity has been searching for an answer to this question across cultures and ages for thousands of years. What is the secret of life? We all catch glimpses and glances through our personal experiences, reflections, education, and choices. But still, we keep asking the question.

Charlie Brown said, "Keep looking up, that's the secret of life." I think the idea is: Be hopeful about the future, things are going to be okay. If life isn't great right now, it will improve. Take a positive outlook. The other option would be to keep looking down, and this negative outlook would probably become a self-fulfilling prophecy.

James Taylor sings, "The secret of life is enjoying the passage of time." It's about immersing ourselves in the present moment. The past is untouchable, and the future is out of reach. Life is here and now, and no matter how hard you try you cannot shift the fabric of time.

Roald Dahl wrote, "The secret of life is to become very, very good at something that is very, very hard to do." Now, I think Dahl was a brilliant and fascinating person, but I have to disagree with him here. This may have been the secret of life for him, but because this may not be possible for everyone, I believe that eliminates it as a viable answer to the broader question.

Peter Kreeft writes, "This is the secret of life: the self lives only by dying, finds its identity (and its happiness) only by self-forgetfulness, self-giving, self-sacrifice, and agape love."

And Mark Twain suggests, "The secret of life is making your vocation your vacation." Again, it would seem to me, that while it is a gloriously attractive idea, the reality is it is not available to everyone. There are many occupations that we need attended to as a society that nobody is ever going to consider a vacation I suspect. Collecting the trash is the commonly cited example, but it is representative of many others.

So, what is the secret of life?

From a biological perspective it could be argued that the secret of life is survival.

From a philosophical perspective the secret of life is often presented as finding meaning and purpose through love, work, friendship, family, education, self-discovery, or serving others. Some philosophers, including the Holocaust survivor Viktor Frankl, have made the case that meaning can even be found in suffering. Childbirth is a clear example. Another is found in the parents who toil tirelessly at jobs they find miserable to support their families. There are other philosophies that would disagree with all of these. Your local cynic may be a philosopher and argue that life is random and cruel and that there is no secret or meaning.

From a spiritual perspective, different religions and spiritual traditions have proposed that the secret of life is enlightenment, compassion and kindness, obedience to God, connection with the divine, relationship with God, union with God, or wholehearted love of God and neighbor.

From a personal perspective, it has been argued that the secret of life is all about having fun, enjoying yourself. Others think pleasure is the secret and purpose of life. Some believe it is finding balance between work and the other aspects of life. And then there is the age-old proposal that the secret of life is success, the accumulation of money and possessions, and the power that comes with all of these.

There is a seemingly endless number of ways to look at life, and myriad thought-provoking answers to the question: What is the secret of life?

When I am preparing to speak at an event, I find it helpful to scribble out a lot of notes, ideas, questions, quotes, and stories. Once I have a sense of the range of possible content, I have a tool I designed years ago to drive maximum clarity. I challenge myself to answer this question in ten words or less: What are you trying to say?

Once I have unearthed the ten words (or less), I test them against another question: One year from now, if the audience remembers just one thing from your presentation, do these ten words represent the one thing you want them to remember?

This little exercise drives intentionality and clarity. It also breeds confidence. But ten words. That's hard. I've hit seven words a few times and that felt good. But the lowest I ever achieved was four. It happened a couple of years back as I was preparing to speak at a fundraiser in Minneapolis.

The organizers had asked me to speak about the secret of life. I didn't like the title at first. I wouldn't have chosen it. But I did what I do, started thinking about it, scribbling notes, reading, praying, and asking others what their thoughts were on the topic.

Standing before the audience a few weeks later, I told them I was going to tell them the secret of life in just four words. Some people laughed. I think they thought it was the beginning of a joke, but I'm also certain their table had been over-served. The rest seemed a little skeptical, but engaged and curious. I had their attention, and the first job of a public speaker is to get everyone's attention at the outset.

What is the secret of life? What are those four words?

Want the right things.

WHAT ARE THE RIGHT THINGS?

Desire directs our lives.

The things we desire add to our joy or destroy our joy. There is a relationship between the quality of your desires and the quality of your life. Is wanting the right things the absolute and definitive secret of life? I don't know. It doesn't matter.

Desire is a critical aspect of our lives, of that I am certain, and that is enough. Many people can, and have, and will, argue that the secret of life is something else. That's okay. What is clear is that desire and what we choose to want plays an enormous role in the unfolding of each human life. That's what we want to explore, seek to understand, and learn to master here. This naturally leads us to ask: What are the right things to want?

If some desires are right, others are wrong. Our culture is increasingly uncomfortable with this idea. This brings us face to face with one of the great dictators of our age: Relativism.

Relativism is a philosophy that asserts there is no absolute truth. It states that nothing is true for everyone. "You have your truth, and I have my truth," we hear people say. This is the abusive fruit of relativism. Relativism aggressively opposes distinctions between right and wrong. The first problem with relativism is the assertion that it is absolutely true that nothing is absolutely true.

If there is no right path, that means all paths are equal, and that is obviously disorienting, especially to the hearts and minds of our young people. But you can see how this could lead us quickly into a philosophical quagmire, so let's not go there.

Let's just say that some desires help you to flourish, and others don't. Some desires help you become the-best-version-of-yourself and others are self-destructive. And some desires are good for other people and other desires would bring harm to others if they were pursued.

What are the right things to desire?

This is a question of discernment. We need to discern which desires to pursue because our desire does not discern. Let me explain. Our faculty of desire is a complex and multifaceted aspect of the human person, but it does not discern between desires that are good or bad for us. It has no moral capacity. It is the function of the soul and the intellect to discern which desires to pursue and which desires to set aside.

Let me explain further. Thinking and desiring are two distinct cognitive processes that operate independently within the mind. Whatever your mind decides to point your desire toward—good or bad—your desire function will work to bring about. It will do everything within its power to bring that desire to fruition. If you fill your mind with a desire for something that is self-destructive it will pursue that desire with the same determination and energy it pursues a desire that is good for you. It doesn't know the difference. That's not its job. There is demarcation between your thinking function and your desiring function.

Our desires need to be discerned before we act upon them for many reasons. Chief among those reasons are: (1) some of our desires lead us to become the-best-version-of-ourselves and others are self-destructive, (2) some of our desires help other people to flourish while others prevent flourishing in other people, (3) we simply have too many desires to pursue them all, and (4) the desires we decide to pursue determine the direction of our lives.

Discernment cannot be rushed. It takes time. The faster our lives are the harder it is to discern. The busier our lives are the harder it is to discern.

Slowing down to the speed of joy is especially important when it comes to discerning desire because desire itself is fast. Every desire manifests within us as urgent. To add to the complexity of our discernment, things we want often present themselves as urgent needs.

Lust is impatient. Not just sexual lust. Lust to eat and drink, lust to shop, for a promotion at work, for material possessions, money and power. Driving fast is a form of lust. Nothing will disconnect you from the speed of joy faster than lust.

Leisure allows us to temper and direct our desires for the best outcome. Speed and busyness don't allow us the reflection needed to step back and discern which desires are good for us and which are self-sabotaging.

What you decide to want impacts everything. Whatever you direct the immense power of your desire toward will grow and expand in your life.

Slowing down to the speed of joy will allow you adequate time to discern which desires to pursue.

Again, this brings us back to our question: What are the right things to desire?

The right things to want are those that lead you and others to flourish. The more we flourish the more we are capable of love. The opposite of flourishing is languishing. It means to lose vitality, to grow weak and feeble. You could be phenomenally successful and at the same time be withering or languishing. You could indulge in one pleasure after another, and those pleasures could be destroying you—body and soul.

You don't need me to make you a list. Somewhere deep inside you know the things that will lead you to flourish and those that will cause you to languish. You may deceive yourself for a day, or a week, or even a year, but in time you will awaken to your self-deception and know the path to flourishing.

What are the right things to want? I know you want a list. I've been trying to avoid lists, but I will relent with some caveats, and I will give you a list.

Some of the right things to want are the same for everyone. Some of the right things to want change with the seasons of our lives. Some we can live without, and others we shouldn't live without (even if we can). Some are deeply personal, just for you type things. You won't find them on this list. The list is not in priority order. It's not in order of most important to least important (or vice versa). It's not in any order at all. The list is not complete or even close to exhaustive. The purpose of the list is simply to give you some examples as a point of reference.

I'm certain I will read this list after publication and be struck by something that is not on the list. I know that will happen because this is going to be a stream-of-consciousness exercise, not a sit-here-and-agonize-for-days-over-the-list exercise. So, here's your list: the right things to desire.

Needs. Wanting what you need is wisdom.

Truth, beauty, and goodness.

Virtue.

Gratitude.

God. A deep unshakable connection.

Heaven. C.S. Lewis observed, "If I find in myself desires which nothing in this world can satisfy, the only logical explanation is that I was made for another world."

Love. Opportunities to love and be loved. To know that you are loved, not because of anything you did, or gave, or even because you loved, but that you are loved just for who you are.

Meaningful relationships.

Sundays. A day of rest.

Friends.

Family.

Leisure.

Joy.

To live your life at the speed of joy.

Dreams.

Beautiful thoughts.

Laughter.

Great books to read. Time to read them.

To know the will of God.

Forgiveness. The grace to forgive. The desire to forgive. The courage to ask for the desire to forgive when you don't want to forgive.

Enthusiasm.

Healing.

A healthy mind.

Patience.

Kindness.

A strong work ethic.

A chance to serve others.

Optimism.

The desire to grow and improve.

Curiosity.

Faith.

Hope.

To be staggeringly generous.

To die peacefully in your sleep at an old age.

To give something away every day.

Clarity. To know what matters most and to be satisfied ignoring what doesn't matter.

Contentment.

Wisdom.

Tears. Tears of joy, tears of healing.

Trust.

Enough. Not more, not less.

To grow old graciously and gracefully.

The very-best-version-of-yourself.

To flourish.

To want the right things for the right reasons.

# # #

What did you think as you read the list?

I just went for a little walk and reread the list when I returned, and what occurred to me is that I cannot buy anything on this list. Money can certainly make some more likely to happen, but they cannot be purchased outright.

Our desires are one of the major sources of our joys and our problems. Wanting the right things, or wanting the wrong things, will have an outsized impact on your life. You can want whatever you want, but the stakes are high, and the consequences are real when it comes to what we choose to focus our desires upon.

It is critical to acknowledge that our desires are not all good for us. Many things we have the capacity to desire can drain and destroy us, prevent us from flourishing, and steal our joy. And the faster and busier your life the more likely you are to want the wrong things.

We are also not victims of our desires. "I fell in love. There was nothing I could do," people sometimes say. This person is saying love is not a conscious choice, I have no agency and therefore no personal responsibility. This person is therefore incapable of respect, commitment, or setting and honoring boundaries. None of these are possible if we allow our emotions to overwhelm us.

We get to choose who we love. We may become infatuated by someone, but infatuation doesn't steal our agency. Love doesn't render us brain dead. We get to decide how we will respond to that infatuation. We get to decide which desires to pursue and which to set aside. We are not victims of desire. This would be a tragic way to live.

Our feelings and desires can be powerful, but we have control over our actions. We are not slaves to our desires. We are free to choose. We have agency and responsibility, and we can exercise self-control.

You get to choose what to direct your desire toward, and that is a powerful ability. A phenomenal ability. This power is at your service every day of your life. If you direct your desire at the right things, even in small matters, this will gradually and then massively change your life.

One lesson I have learned the hard way is that wanting things that aren't good for you complicates your life. It may sound simple, but life is difficult enough as it is. Don't complicate your life. Want the things that make you flourish.

Direct your desire toward things that your future self will thank you for wanting.

THE WISDOM OF ENOUGH

Shelter Island is one hundred miles east of Manhattan, nestled between the North and South forks of Long Island. Known for its natural beauty and its breathtaking hiking, biking, and kayaking, it consists of a mere twenty-seven square miles and is only accessible by ferry. While it boasts a small number of permanent residents, the summer months swell the population as it becomes a playground for the rich and famous.

John Bogle was the legendary investor who founded the Vanguard Group, popularized the index fund, and was a hero to the little guy. He believed in investment rather than speculation, long-term patience over short term action, and he was an ardent advocate of reducing broker fees. To summarize his investment philosophy, he believed the best investment vehicle was a low-cost index fund, held over a lifetime with dividends reinvested.

Bogle was fond of telling this true story which took place at a party on Shelter Island.

Two friends were enjoying the party when their host, a billionaire hedge fund manager, entered the room. Joseph Heller was well-known for his novel *Catch-22*. Published in forty languages, it was one of the bestselling novels of its time. Kurt Vonnegut was his friend, and a successful author of fourteen novels and five plays himself.

As their host made his way around the room, Kurt Vonnegut informed his friend that their host had made more money in a single day than Heller had earned from his wildly popular novel *Catch-22* over its whole history.

"Yes, but I have something he will never have," Heller responded.

"What's that?" Vonnegut inquired.

"Enough," Heller replied "Enough."

In telling the story, John Bogle added, "*Enough.* I was stunned by the simple eloquence of that word—stunned for two reasons: First, because I have been given so much in my own life and, second, because Joseph

Heller couldn't have been more accurate. For a critical element of our society, including many of the wealthiest and most powerful among us, there seems to be no limit today on what *enough* entails."

While I would like to have a broader conversation about enough, all these men were speaking about money, and that is as good as any other place to start our conversation. Money is certainly one of the main drivers of the joyless urgency that has a firm grip on the throat of our culture.

My own experience spending time with the wealthy has led me to believe that those who have the most money seem least adept at determining how much is enough. When asked, "How much is enough?" I have heard many who already had enough for several lifetimes joke, "Just a little bit more." And while it may seem humorous to some, it is, as we will soon discover, profoundly sad.

Do you have a number? While 37% of Americans have nothing saved for retirement, a popular conversation on Wall Street, and among successful business owners around the world, surrounds what is referred to as "the number." Your number is the amount of money you would need to walk away and live comfortably for the rest of your life.

The number has more to do with ego than anything else for most of these people. Many successful entrepreneurs have set a number and changed it many times. When they first hear about "the number" they set a number that is more than enough, but once they reach that number, they increase "their number" to an even more ludicrous amount. And when they surpass that number, they increase it again.

Don't misunderstand me. There is nothing wrong with having financial goals. They are laudable in fact. It is the underlying aspirations and motivations that are often found wanting.

Financial planners preparing clients for retirement also encourage clients to calculate a number. The key word here is calculate. While many of the people discussed above allow their egos to pluck a number out of the ether, responsible financial professionals help clients to calculate a number based in reality.

Some people will say it's impossible to predict how much money you will need in the future. This is true in a sense, because you may encounter unexpected expenses like long-term care, or inflation may stay above its historical average for a long period of time, or you may have a child with special needs. But, while it is impossible to predict exactly how much money you will need in the future, it is possible to estimate how much you are likely to need and build in some margin.

The simplest form of this calculation involves determining your annual living expenses and multiplying by twenty, which will give you the total amount of investable assets needed to support a 5% annual withdrawal. For example, if your annual living expenses are $50,000, your number would be $50,000 x 20 = $1,000,000. This is your number.

There are a number of factors that can increase or decrease the number. If you expect to receive $2,000 each month from Social Security, a pension, or from continuing to work part-time, the number would be considerably lower. With annual living expenses of $50,000, minus $24,000 income, leaves a future need of $26,000 annually, multiplied by 20 equals $520,000, and that is your number.

A dynamic model would build in a 3% annual increase in expenses to allow for inflation, and you may be encouraged to add some margin for peace of mind. And for the sake of simplicity this example assumes annual taxes are included in the calculation of annual expenses.

How much money is enough? It is possible to gauge this with some analysis, but less than 10% of Americans under the age of sixty-five have ever performed this simple calculation.

The point I wish to make is that very few of us know how much is enough. The demonstration was in financial terms, but in all aspects of life, most of us do not know how much is enough. The result of this self-imposed ignorance is that we perpetually think we don't have enough.

We eat too much. Drink too much. Work too much. Worry too much. Talk too much. Consume too much. Waste too much. Compare too much. Expect too much. Resent too much. Schedule too much. Judge too much. Multitask too much. Criticize too much. Blame too much. Shop too much. Stress too much. Isolate too much. Binge-watch too much. Ruminate too much. Gamble too much. Pamper too much. Get angry too much. Waste time too much. Overindulge too much. Shame too much. Envy too much. Expose too much. Rush too much. Fear too much.

We're not good at enough.

We excel at too much and it isn't something to excel at.

Enough is a beautiful word. It's a soul-captivating word. It's time to trade our excess for enough. Enough signifies balance, harmony, sufficiency, and contentment. It symbolizes the state between lack and excess.

One of the primary reasons we don't slow down is because we don't think we *have* enough. One of the main reasons we are excessively busy is because we don't think we *are* enough.

Knowing that you have enough, that you are enough—here, now, to-day—is essential to slowing down to the speed of joy.

With each passing year we can recklessly increase the speed of our lives or graciously slow to the speed of joy. I heard a sixty-fifth birthday celebration speech recently that borrows from a number of sources and provides the perspective of a lifetime:

"What a glorious night. Every face I see is a memory. It may not be a perfect memory. We've had our ups and downs. There has been plenty of laughter, and there have been tears. Broken hearts and bruised egos. We've misunderstood each other and argued at times, but we've had a lifetime of conversations and those conversations have challenged and encouraged me—and I thank you for that. I may not have been grateful at the time, but I am grateful tonight. My life is richer for having known you. You have each in your own inimitable way made me a better man.

And now, here we are, all together, face to face, in one place, after all these years, and you're mine for a night. Time has slowed to give us this moment. And I'm going to break precedent and tell you my one candle wish.

That you would have a life as blessed and as lucky as mine, where you can wake up one morning and say, 'I don't want anything more.' Not because life was easy, it wasn't, and not because life was always fair, it wasn't, and not because of all my success and the treasure that has come with that, but because life itself is enough.

I've had my heart broken and I've been brutally betrayed, you know that. It's been no secret. But you get yourself up, dust yourself off, and you press on. That's life. I've also had many of those moments that take your breath away and fill you with awe and wonder. Those moments have taught me that all is gift. There's nothing we can do to merit life's most precious moments. They are pure gift. And these are life too. We don't deserve them, but God gives them to us anyway—unconditionally and unreservedly.

But more than anything else, after all these years, we still have each other. You came tonight to celebrate me, but I am here to celebrate you. Without you, I would not be the man I am today; without you, I would not have had the success I have enjoyed. You've loved me and you've allowed me to love you—and that has been the privilege of my life. And for that I thank you with all my heart.

Sixty-five years, don't they go by in a blink?"

# # #

We have so much to learn from our elders. Ralph Waldo Emerson observed, "The years teach much that the days never knew."

Do you remember the one candle wish? "That you would have a life as blessed and as lucky as mine, where you can wake up one morning and say, 'I don't want anything more.'"

What would have to happen for you to get to that place? What would have to change for you to be able to wake each morning and say, "I don't want anything more." When will that day be for you?

There are two ways to get there. The first way is to get more. More of what? I don't know. It's different for everyone. More love, more money, more health, more security, more friends, more status, more stuff. More. The second way is to get content.

You may not have enough of everything for the rest of your life, but you have enough of a lot of things for today. What do you have enough of today? Live in the awareness that you don't need anything more today. And more importantly—you are enough.

Live in the wisdom of enough. Slowing down to the speed of joy gets easier the more we realize we have enough and that we are enough.

A thousand years before the birth of Jesus, King David was reflecting on the wisdom of enough, and these are the conclusions he arrived at:

The Lord is my shepherd, there is nothing I shall want.
He lets me lie down in green pastures.
He leads me beside peaceful waters.
He restores my soul.
He guides me along the way of righteousness as befits his name.
Even though I walk through the valley of the shadow of death,
I will not be afraid.
For the Lord is at my side.
His rod and his staff comfort and protect me.
He prepares a table for me in the presence of my enemies.
He anoints my head with oil.
My cup overflows.

*Surely goodness and mercy will follow me all the days of my life.
And I will live in the house of the Lord, forever.*

# # #

Enoughness is a beautiful thing.

A CRISIS OF CONTENTMENT

The wisdom of enough is far from the hearts and minds of modern men and women. There is a growing sense of dissatisfaction in people's lives today, despite unprecedented levels of education, individual freedom, technological advancement, convenience, healthcare and longevity, infrastructure, global mobility, and material wealth. How can people who have so much be so dissatisfied?

The people of our age are dissatisfied with their circumstances. This is the very definition of discontentment. We are living in the age of discontent.

The average American lives better than Alexander the Great, Queen Victoria, King Louis XIV, Genghis Khan, Catherine the Great, Charlemagne, King Solomon, and Emperor Augustus.

The quality of our lives is greater than ever, and yet, the rise of depression, anxiety, and suicide is unprecedented. So perhaps the experts are using the wrong criteria to measure quality of life.

We live in an age crippled by discontentment. Contentment is commonly defined as a state of happiness and satisfaction, but happiness and satisfaction seem too fleeting. I would describe contentment as a profound sense of fulfillment and soul gratification. Why do we have so little of it?

Enough + Gratitude = Contentment.

We have enough but don't acknowledge it.

Gratitude is the missing ingredient. Ingratitude is cancer of the soul. Ingratitude is ugly.

Ungrateful people tend to be miserable and resentful, and they are exhausting and toxic to be around. Ingratitude is a denial of reality. Ingratitude is a destroyer of relationships.

Grateful people are universally loved, while the ungrateful are secretly despised. Jane Austen observed, "There is no vice so mean as ingratitude, and it is what I detest in others." But Austen might change her mind if she were alive today, because there is something more insidious eating away at the hearts and souls of modern men and women: Entitlement. Entitlement is the belief that one is inherently deserving of privileges and special treatment, and it is at the core of the restlessness and dissatisfaction plaguing our times.

The opposite of gratitude is entitlement. Entitlement is a state of perpetual disappointment. It always leaves you wanting for more. It's a spiritual and emotional black hole. Entitlement is a path to loneliness and dissatisfaction.

The more you think you are entitled to something, the less you will be satisfied with it. William Shakespeare observed that, "Expectations are the root of all heartache" and entitlement is an unreasonable and unrealistic expectation that can never be met.

A person possessed by entitlement is incapable of being grateful. Anything that diminishes gratitude will increase dissatisfaction. Entitlement and unhappiness are synonymous. If you think life owes you something, you will end up feeling cheated.

Gratitude cures so much restlessness and dissatisfaction.

It's impossible to be grateful and unhappy at the same time. Satisfaction and gratitude go hand in hand. Happiness and gratitude are inseparable. There are no happy ungrateful people and there are no happy entitled people.

And unhappiness is not the only dark spirit that gratitude casts out. Try being grateful and angry at the same time. Try being grateful and jealous at the same time.

Try being grateful and bitter, resentful, impatient, irritable, bored, hostile, stingy, antagonistic, unkind, or disrespectful at the same time. It isn't possible. Gratitude must be set aside to take on these negative dispositions.

Gratitude is the virtue of rejoicing in what is. It is the quality of being thankful. It expresses appreciation for all that is good, true, and beautiful in our lives. Gratitude is a simple acknowledgement of reality. It is a form of wisdom.

Gratitude is deeply rooted in humility. The grateful recognize that all is gift—our talents, experiences, relationships, opportunities, and the world around us. All is gift.

The enough mindset facilitates gratitude. Gratitude is the path that leads to contentment. And contentment is a soothing balm for the soul of our age.

We are losing ourselves in the never-ending quest for more. Slowing down to the speed of joy will allow you to immerse yourself in the enough mindset. The enough mindset releases gratitude and gratitude gives birth to contentment. Otherwise, we will continue to undermine our priorities and compromise our values in pursuit of getting more and more of what we don't need.

Foster a deep sense of gratitude.

What are you grateful for today?

Who are you grateful for today?

What's the best thing that happened to you today?

What is bringing you joy during this season of your life?

What made you smile today?

Who was the last person who made you laugh?

What material possession have you delighted in recently?

Who has had a profound impact on your life?

What's one thing you're thankful for that you tend to overlook?

What small blessing have you been marveling at of late?

What's the best conversation you've had this year?

What's your fondest memory from last year?

Who has cared for you most in this lifetime?

When did you last delight in the beauty of nature?

Reflect on a time when you felt deeply appreciated.

Reflect on an unexpected happening that changed your life for the better.

Reflect on a moment of contentment in your life.

Reflect on the people who have helped you pursue your dreams.

Whose generosity and goodness inspire you?

What has happened recently that reminded you how fortunate you are?

What simple pleasure are you looking forward to today?

Enough + Gratitude = Contentment.

IN SEARCH OF THE VITAL FEW

Slowing down to the speed of joy is a quest for the vital few.

It is time to throw off the trivial many and embrace the vital few in every aspect of our lives. The key to this quest is to identify what is essential and focus on that. The vital few will liberate you from the insane busyness of the modern world. Those few things that really matter. This is known as essentialism.

80% of consequences come from 20% of causes. This was Vilfredo Pareto's theory, which has been applied in almost every way imaginable since his discovery in 1897. This theory is also known as the 80/20 Principle, and it has provided staggering insight into thousands of aspects of our lives.

Examples in our personal lives:

We wear 20% of our clothes 80% of the time.

20% of our decisions account for 80% of our happiness or misery.

20% of our relationships provide 80% of our support and satisfaction.

20% of your carpet has 80% of the wear.

20% of our purchases are responsible for 80% of our financial strain.

20% of our habits account for 80% of our well-being.

20% of our tasks produce 80% of the results.

Examples at work include:

80% of a company's sales come from 20% of its customers.

20% of the tasks in an organization account for 80% of the results.

20% of clients account for 80% of revenue.

20% of products are responsible for 80% of profits and customer complaints (not necessarily the same 20%).

We use 20% of a tech-product's features 80% of the time.

20% of employees contribute 80% of the results.

Examples in society at large:

20% of countries contribute 80% of global GDP.

20% of criminals are responsible for 80% of crimes.

20% of patients are responsible for 80% of healthcare costs.

20% of donors contribute 80% of donations.

20% of countries are responsible for 80% of global carbon emissions.

20% of the world's population consumes 80% of the world's resources.

20% of businesses generate 80% of jobs.

# # #

The examples are endless. The theory is an invitation to focus on what is essential. Identifying the 20% (the vital few) and focusing on them rather than the 80% (the trivial many) is crucial to success in almost every aspect of life.

The lesson here traditionally has been to encourage people to focus on these high-impact activities that yield massive results, so they can do and accomplish more. I am proposing something very different. Focus on the high-impact activities that yield massive results, so you can have more leisure time.

The first step is to identify the vital few.

What is essential? This question has given rise to the essentialism movement. What is essentialism? Author Greg McKeown describes it as "the disciplined pursuit of less" and goes on to explain, "The way of the essentialist involves doing less, but better, so you can make the highest possible contribution. The way of the essentialist isn't about getting more done in less time. It's not about getting less done. It's about getting only the right things done. It's about challenging the core assumption of 'we can have it all' and 'I have to do everything' and replacing it with the pursuit of 'the right thing, in the right way, at the right time.' Essentialism is about regaining control of our own choices about where to spend our time and energies instead of giving others implicit permission to choose for us."

Let's face a truth: You cannot do everything. It's a lie that we have been tormenting ourselves with for far too long, a multi-generational myth that is robbing us of our joy on a daily basis.

Imagine doing less and accomplishing more. Not a little bit more, but 3 times, 5 times, 10 times, 16 times. Imagine doing less and having more impact. This is the path to the fulfillment and contentment you have been yearning for all your life.

So, the question isn't actually: What is essential? The question is: What is essential for you?

There is no one-size-fits-all answer. It is a deeply personal question and requires a deeply personal answer. Deeply personal questions require reflection, and reflection requires leisure.

What is essential for you? That is an answer only you can find by delving into your life and spending ample time reflecting on five big questions: Who are you? Why are you here? How do you do it? What matters most? What matters least?

Abandon the trivial many and embrace the vital few.

WE WANT SO MUCH AND NEED SO LITTLE

We want so much and need so little. This is a powerful truth and one that most of us struggle to grasp. But few things will prevent you from slowing down to the speed of joy more than material possessions. Stuff weighs us down. It rents space in our minds. Acquiring things and maintaining our stuff both rob us of valuable leisure time.

My most powerful experience with this truth was many years ago when I walked the Camino de Santiago. It's an ancient walking path that begins in the south of France, crosses the Pyrenees mountains, and then crosses directly west across northern Spain to Santiago de Compostela. Stretching just over five hundred miles, pilgrims have been walking the path since at least the ninth century.

Modern day pilgrims are encouraged to carry a pack of no more than twenty pounds for the forty-day walk (which I planned to complete in twenty-one days). I remember looking at everything neatly laid out on my bed before I put everything into my backpack. I remember wondering how I was ever going to get by with so little. But by the end of the second day, I was giving things away that I knew I wouldn't need to people in the villages along the way. It was clear by the end of the second day that many of the things I brought were superfluous.

Our lives are full of superfluous stuff. Things that are superfluous are unnecessary, excessive, redundant, irrelevant, or simply more than we need.

We need so little. Walking the Camino I would look at my backpack each night and shake my head. Things I thought were crucial a few days earlier were now unnecessary, and more than that, they were a burden because I had to carry them every day.

Pilgrimage is a paradigm for life. So much of what we think is essential is unnecessary, but we won't discover that unless we slow down for long enough to reflect. Reflection allows us to recognize the insanity of our lives, so we can set out to realign our lives with our values and priorities.

The wisdom of enough reveals that so much of the speed and busyness of our lives is driven by a desire to acquire more stuff that is completely unnecessary.

The wisdom of enough encourages us to unburden ourselves of the stuff that we don't need. Not all of it. Some things bring us great joy and they should be cherished, but most things distract us from living.

Over the past five years, as I've worked on slowing down to embrace the speed of joy, I've also been on a mission to simplify my life. Everywhere I turned, I encountered the same message: "Simplify your life." This process of slowing down opened my eyes to how much unnecessary stuff I had—and how it was weighing me down and pulling my focus away from what truly matters.

Around that time, I published a book called *The Generosity Habit.*

"The generosity habit is simple: Give something away every day. It doesn't need to be money or material things. In fact, the philosophy behind the generosity habit rests on this singular truth: You don't need money or material possessions to live a life of staggering generosity."

The book was about creative generosity: Express your appreciation. Call someone you haven't spoken to in a while. Catch someone doing something right. Plant a tree. Do something to make another person's day. Teach. Coach. Encourage. Smile. Visit someone who is lonely. Support a local business. Bring people together. Compliment a stranger. Be a generous lover. Give blood. Invite someone to share their hopes and dreams with you. Listen deeply.

I wanted to demonstrate that we can live lives of staggering generosity even if we have no money or things to give to others. But just after the book was published, I felt challenged to start giving material possessions away. So, I set about to give away one physical item every day for a year.

The year came and went. It was great fun. But I still had far too much stuff, so I decided to keep going. In a few weeks it will have been three years since I started giving a material possession away every day—and I still have too much stuff.

I'm going to keep giving my stuff away. It's a lot of fun. But it's harder than you think. To give the right thing to the right person requires some intentionality.

Letting go of stuff that we don't need can be unbelievably liberating. The freedom that comes from simplifying our lives is amazing.

A lot of the hurry and hustle in our lives is generated by the things we own or the things we want to own. Once we discover how little we need, and the real cost of owning and maintaining things, we can step back and rethink our approach.

This leads us to the realization that less really can be more.

Less is more. The first time we believe this to be true is a significant moment in our journey. We may take steps forward and steps backward after that day, but over time we will gravitate back to the truth that less is more and align our lives with that truth.

THE RIGHT AMOUNT OF ANYTHING

The right amount of anything makes all the difference.

Too much sugar in your coffee and it is spoiled. Too much salt on food and a dish could go from being delicious to disgusting. Overexpose a photograph and it looks bland and details become lost. Overcooked food can be burnt on the outside and undercooked on the inside. And you cannot walk these things back. You can't remove sugar from coffee, extract salt from food, unexpose a photograph, or uncook food. The effects of too much cannot be reversed, undone, or corrected (in these examples and many more). There is no way to salvage or remedy these situations.

Too much is dangerous, but we seem intent on finding out just how much is too much in many aspects of our lives.

One of the greatest pieces of modern insanity is FOMO—Fear of Missing Out. The reality is we miss out on almost everything. Just try not to miss out on the things God intended just for you.

The idea that if we make the right choices, squeeze enough into each day, and become ultra-efficient, we won't miss out on anything is a colossal error. More than an error, it is a delusion. We are going to miss out. We miss out on almost everything. And that's okay. That's as it should be. But knowing the right amount of anything transforms FOMO into JOMO—the Joy of Missing Out.

Living at the speed of joy helps us to recognize the right amount.

When I took my seat on the plane last week, I realized I was sitting next to a Catholic priest. We got to talking and after a while the topic of Confession came up. He shared he has been a priest for twenty-five years and I asked him, "What has surprised you about hearing confessions for all those years?"

"People don't confess their greed," he explained. I asked him if he was saying that greed was one of the least confessed sins and he corrected me saying, "In twenty-five years nobody has ever confessed to being greedy."

Never. Nobody had ever confessed to being greedy. I found that fascinating.

Greed is an intense and selfish desire for more of something than you need. It goes beyond a healthy ambition. It signifies a lack of contentment and an inability to be content. Greed is a continuous self-centered craving for more. It can easily lead to the idolatry of wealth (or the object of greed), misuse of resources, and moral corruption. Greed is a form of spiritual poverty. It is a manifestation of the disordered priorities of someone who prioritizes the material over the spiritual and self above others.

The right amount of anything is the key to contentment, but greed isn't interested in the right amount of anything, it is only interested in more. Greed is an enemy of contentment.

When we were doing our research on generosity a few years back, I was similarly struck to discover that nobody considers themselves to be cheap, miserly, or stingy (except those that take pride in it).

I have also never met anyone who thought they had too much money. The thought never seems to occur to some of the wealthiest. But there must be an amount beyond which money becomes less of a help and more of a burden. And I have never met anyone who thought they had the right amount of money. Lots of people believe they need more, some are honest enough to say they just want more, and some think they are entitled to more. Most think they deserve more. I've never met anyone who thought they had too much power or influence. I've never met anyone who thought they gave too much unsolicited advice, I've never met a manager who confessed to being a micromanager, and King Solomon for all his wisdom had seven hundred wives. That seems a little excessive.

Our ability to measure the right amount and govern ourselves to that right amount doesn't seem to be functioning. This is the result of psychological factors, social expectations and pressures, and cultural influences. But it is also the result of a lack of leisure-born reflection. This lack of reflection allows us to continue deceiving ourselves and being deceived by the culture. For example, our inability to set aside the "more is always better" doctrine is the result of how deeply ingrained it is in our culture, but it is also the result of our lack of reflection.

The instrument inside us that calculates how much is enough is malfunctioning. It needs repairs. These repairs naturally occur through the consistent and disciplined practice of daily reflection and a leisurely observance of the Sabbath.

The habit of quiet reflection reveals aspects of ourselves, the world, and other people that would otherwise remain hidden to us. Remember for a moment how Pieper defined leisure, "Leisure is an attitude of mind and a condition of the soul that fosters a capacity to receive the reality of the world." This is what happens through the habit of quiet reflection, and by extension we become less susceptible to deception. Reflection allows us to notice things about ourselves, the world, and other people that would otherwise remain hidden.

The daily habit of reflection maximizes our ability to learn from our experiences, both positive and negative. Quiet reflection gives rise to a heightened awareness of self that provides penetrating insight into our motives, desires, feelings, emotional patterns, strengths, weaknesses, hopes and fears, and the threats and opportunities that are looming.

Quiet reflection helps us identify how much is the right amount.

There is a right amount of anything. Some people may claim that it is impossible to know how much the right amount is. I disagree. It may elude you. It may require effort, investigation, and honest reflection to arrive at it, but there is an ideal amount. A Boston dentist named William T.G. Morton used sulfuric ether to anesthetize a man who needed surgery to remove a tumor from his neck on October 16, 1846. This was the first use of anesthesia and the optimal dose of anesthesia has been continually refined ever since, making it safer and more effective with every passing decade.

There is an optimal amount of anything.

There is an optimal amount of salt in your favorite meal.

There is an optimal amount of sleep. If you got exactly that amount of sleep each night you would thrive beyond comprehension.

There is an optimal amount of stuff for you to own. Beyond that amount of stuff, it becomes a distraction and burden, requires maintenance and space, starts producing stress and anxiety, and erects a barrier to human flourishing.

There is an amount of money beyond which you cease becoming a-better-version-of-yourself.

It may be different for each person, but just as sure as you know when there is too much salt in your food, you would know if you exceeded that amount of money.

There is an optimal amount of time for you to work each day.

There is an amount of screentime beyond which you become less patient, more impulsive, experience eye strain, have difficulty falling asleep, experience more anxiety and depression, suffer from diminished attention span, and begin to display compulsive behavior.

There is an optimal amount of time for you to spend in quiet reflection each day.

And the right amount of anything can make all the difference.

More isn't always the answer. It is time to set aside our bias toward more. Our default setting is more and that is hurting us. There is such a thing as too much. How much is too much? The amount of anything that prevents you from flourishing. Any amount that becomes an obstacle to the-best-version-of-yourself is too much. Jesus counseled us, "If your right eye causes you to sin, tear it out and throw it away. . . And if your right hand causes you to sin, cut it off and throw it away" (Matthew 5:29-30). What we are discussing here is challenging but nowhere near as difficult as what Jesus is proposing, and yet the same spirit is at work in both.

When something of this world stops serving you, prevents you from flourishing, or worse still, prevents you from making progress, cast it away from you. Whether it be money or things, food or your phone, a toxic person or group of friends, social media or the speed and busyness of life, if it isn't helping you to be all that God created you to be. . . throw it far away from you.

There is such a thing as too much. We should be calculating it. We should be paying more attention to it in many areas of our lives. The "more is better myth" is destroying our lives. It needs to be crushed. Obliterated. There is a right amount of anything. There is such a thing as enough. These realizations are the gateway to contentment.

Knowing what to want, learning how to be content, discovering what the vital few are for you (and your family), realizing how little we actually need and that there is a right amount of anything. These are all powerful lessons that make it easier to slow down to the speed of joy, but the best is yet to come.

THE GREAT CLARIFIER

What if you're not sure?

The right amount can be difficult to determine in many situations, but in one crucial aspect of our lives the right amount is crystal clear. I have intentionally held off discussing this aspect of the speed and busyness of our lives until now. This is an indispensable piece of the equation when it comes to slowing down to the speed of joy. It impacts everything we do every day.

Time. There are twenty-four hours in each day. It is the same for everyone. It doesn't matter how much money you have—you cannot buy extra hours. It doesn't matter how talented, smart, powerful, or connected you are—you still get twenty-four hours.

Time is the great clarifier. It puts emotions, opinions, and situations into perspective. It reveals our true values and priorities. It reveals outcomes and consequences. Time reveals the layers of a relationship or situation until we see them for what they are. Time is a wise teacher who challenges us to grow and prepares us for the future.

Now let's reflect on some of the things people say and what they really mean.

"I don't have enough time."

You don't have enough time for what? Are you saying God didn't give you enough time?

"I can't keep up."

You can't keep up with what? We can't keep up with our own lives? If our lives are moving so fast that we cannot keep up, what is that telling us? Our approach must be fundamentally flawed.

"There aren't enough hours in the day."

Aren't enough hours for what? If there aren't enough hours in a day to get everything done, the logical question would seem to be: What are you attempting to do that you should not be doing?

"There's just too much on my plate."

Is God expecting you to do more than is reasonable? Has God put an impossible amount on your schedule? Or have you put things on your plate that God never intended for you?

"I'm always behind schedule."

What is that telling you? Always? How long has this been going on? When will you get the message? If you are always behind schedule, you're like one of those dogs chasing a car, but the car is your life.

"I wish I had more hours in a day."

Really? You would like to change God's design of the universe? Our insanity is matched by our arrogance. Or could it be that our insanity is the result of our arrogance?

"There are only twenty-four hours in a day."

Only? The design is perfect. The problem is user error.

# # #

These sayings are a testament to the stress and frustration most people feel every day. The busyness of our lives makes us feel like there isn't enough time to take care of everything.

The origins of the word busy includes a fascinating reference to the term *busybody* which was first used about five hundred years ago. The description reads, "active and meddling in that which does not concern one." There are twenty-four hours in a day, so if we have more to do than can reasonably be done by one person in that period of time, it is logical to conclude that we are "active and meddling in that which does not concern us."

I will be the first to admit that I find myself in this quandary far too often, even during these years where I have been intentionally trying to slow down to the speed of joy. So, it seems many of us are *busybodies* and overly active and meddling in that which does not concern us. We can argue about how much is the right amount of stuff to own or how much is the optimal amount of money for you to thrive. We can disagree about these things. But when it comes to time there is no disagreement. There is nothing to argue about. That would be a disagreement with God. It would be a disagreement with the whole universe.

And here's the thing: We are wrestling with the whole universe when we participate in the inhumane speed and busyness of life that our culture wants to shackle us with. We are trying to stretch the fabric of reality and it cannot be stretched. Reality is inflexible. It will not bend for you, me, or anyone—it will break anyone who doesn't get the message and continues to try.

Time is never punishing you. It is preparing you.

What is the right amount of time? How much is enough time? The right amount of time is twenty-four hours a day. This is indisputable. We know that for sure. If more were needed, it would have been provided.

Most people don't think they have enough time, but this is categorically false. We have exactly enough time to do what we should be doing.

We don't have enough time to waste time, and we all waste plenty of it.

We don't have time to procrastinate.

We don't have time for our self-destructive behaviors, and we don't have time for our unhealthy habits. Bad habits are a waste of time.

We don't have time to lose our temper.

We don't have time to be selfish.

We don't have time to get angry or jealous.

We don't have time to hold a grudge or blame others.

We don't have time to be passive aggressive, sarcastic, possessive, controlling, manipulative, insecure, or resentful.

We don't have time to criticize others.

We don't have time to make bad decisions.

We don't have time to feel sorry for ourselves, throw pity parties, feel insecure, or wallow in self-loathing.

We don't have time for hangovers.

We don't have time for our guilty pleasures.

We don't have time for rivalries.

We don't have time for comparing ourselves to anyone else.

We don't have time for self-criticism, controlling behavior, insecurity, judging self, judging others, arrogance, unresolved guilt, or shame.

And we certainly don't have time for impossibility thinking. We are people of possibility.

We don't have time to be victims. We could waste our whole lives being victims.

We don't have time for ego-based perfectionism.

We don't have time to do a whole bunch of things half-heartedly.

We don't have time to gossip. You just don't have time for that.

We don't have time to fear making a mistake. You are going to make mistakes, that's part of life. Pride gives birth to inaction and the wrong actions.

We don't have time for the obligations we invented. We don't have time to pretend we are more important than we are. We don't have time to go out of our way to get noticed. And we don't have time to worry about what anyone else thinks about us.

How much time did you spend in sin today? We don't have time to sin. God didn't build that into our schedules.

We don't have time for our obsessive-compulsive preferences.

We don't have time for all the things our egos overcommitted us to.

On average, Americans spend seven hours a day on the internet, three hours a day watching television, and touch their iPhones an average of 2,365 times a day. We don't have time for that.

We need to stop worshiping at the altar of more. We don't have enough time for that.

The cult of more has brainwashed us. Efficiency has taken possession of the human psyche, convincing us there are an endless number of ways to get more done. We have become addicted to more, and like all addictions, it has an insatiable appetite and deforms our worldview. It distorts our view of time. Tells us what has value and what is worthless. This cult of efficiency doesn't value leisure. It thinks prayer and reflection are worthless because it looks like you are doing nothing. "Don't just sit there doing nothing, get up and do something." That's what the efficiency demon says to us when it sees us praying, meditating, reflecting, and even reading. It doesn't value long conversations with friends and family.

We have too much of all the wrong things and not enough of all the things that lead human beings to flourish. We can thank the speed and busyness of our lives for that. But we can do something about it.

Let me tell you what you have plenty of time for.

There is plenty of time to love, and plenty of time to listen.

There is time enough to live out the great human mandate our God has placed upon our lives.

There is time for wholeheartedness. Plenty of time to love the Lord your God with your whole heart and your whole mind and your whole soul. And plenty of time to love your neighbor as yourself—wholeheartedly.

There is time to flourish and time to bask in contentedness.

There is plenty of time to be grateful.

There is time to be staggeringly generous.

You just don't have time to do everything your ego wants you to do.

You have plenty of time to do the will of God. Plenty.

You don't need more time. Cast that deception aside. If you needed more time God would have given you more time.

More time isn't the answer. The answer is: careful selection, prayerful discernment, a grateful heart, and acknowledgment of the reality of our finitude.

Stop wrestling with reality. Reality always wins.

Twenty-four hours a day is enough time.

A NEW SPRINGTIME

Spring is nature's celebration of hope. It's a time of renewal and awakening. The whole world flourishes in the spring. It's the season of new beginnings that breathes new life into the whole world.

Do you need a new springtime? A new beginning? A fresh start? I needed one a few years back and I didn't even know it.

I have a feeling your season of hope is just beginning. Albert Camus discovered, "In the midst of winter, I found there was, within me, an invincible summer." There's an invincible summer within you too, but first comes spring—and this is your springtime.

We all yearn for spring. We hunger for new beginnings and second chances. There is a striking quote from *A Moveable Feast*, Hemingway's scattered memoir about his time in Paris as a struggling writer in the 1920s.

"When spring came, even the false spring, there were no problems except where to be happiest. The only thing that could spoil a day was people and if you could keep from making engagements, each day had no limits. People were always the limiters of happiness except for the very few that were as good as spring itself."

This quote has stirred something deep within me over the past five years. I have returned to it time and again.

"Where to be happiest."

"If you keep from making engagements."

"People were always the limiters of happiness."

"Except for the very few that were as good as spring itself."

Now it's time for a new springtime in your life.

It's time to take back your life. It's time for your very own quiet revolution. It all begins with the inner attitude of slowing down. We question simple solutions because we have a bias toward complexity. But our lives need simple solutions. They are already too complex. Slow down and keep in mind, springtime is effortless. It bursts forth.

The world is moving so fast, but you don't have to.

This book is an invitation to slow down. I hope you found it helpful. Its core message really is very simple: Slowing down will change your life.

I promise you, if you just slow down, keep from overcrowding your schedule, allow your priorities to be rearranged, and set the matters of this world aside for one day each week, you will experience miracles in your own life. Miracles.

Albert Einstein's perspective was, "There are only two ways to live your life. One is as though nothing is a miracle. The other is as though everything is a miracle." And C.S. Lewis noted, "Miracles are a retelling in small letters of the very same story which is written across the whole world in letters too large for some of us to see."

It's time to begin construction on the life you cannot wait to wake up to each day.

This is your new springtime.

I want you to know it is possible. I needed a new springtime in my life five years ago. I was on the dark side of the moon. I needed a miracle. I found it by slowing down to the speed of joy. In this book I have shared many of the lessons I learned along the way. But there were three deeply personal lessons, and I saved them for this moment.

The first is wholeheartedness.

Before I discovered the speed of joy there were so many things I didn't even attempt to do wholeheartedly. I was always juggling several things at once, which kept me from excelling at any of them. It also kept me from doing anything wholeheartedly.

Half-hearted living is exhausting, and I was doing everything half-heartedly.

In the opening pages of this book, I shared that if I could go back and live my life over again, I would change the speed at which I have lived my life. I would slow my life down radically. The thing is, I rushed through so many magical moments. I was in an insane hurry. I was so preoccupied with whatever was next, that I dashed through moments, and missed out on fully experiencing them.

Growing up in the suburbs of anywhere, children have all sorts of dreams. But a life like this, the one I've been blessed to live, would have seemed preposterous. It defies logic and probability. It would have been impossible to imagine the life I have lived when I was a child. And I could never have anticipated the journey I was embarking on as a speaker and an author at the age of nineteen.

Words cannot capture the gratitude that fills my heart when I reflect on my life. It is humbling. I don't know why God chose me. I was given talents and abilities, I followed them, and this is where they led. I don't know why I was given those gifts. The ways of God are a mystery.

But there is one thing I know: As a teenager, in the suburbs of Sydney, I surrendered my life to God, and this is what he did.

There is also an unsettling truth I have had to face: I wasn't fully present for so many remarkable moments along the way. And that makes me sad.

We can only *fully* experience each moment of life at the speed of joy. At any other speed we miss out. When we rush anything, we don't get to *fully* experience the great and small moments that make up our lives.

Presence is a gift. It's one we all love to receive. It's a gift I'm trying to get better at giving. When we give someone our undivided attention and engage that person in a meaningful way, we demonstrate in a very practical sense that we love, value, and respect that person. When we don't, people feel unloved, undervalued, and disrespected.

Our greatest ability is our availability. Slowing down to the speed of joy has taught me to make myself wholeheartedly available to people. It has taught me to resist distractions, set aside any preoccupations that float through my mind, and make the effort to be intentionally present to people physically, emotionally, intellectually, and spiritually.

The speed of joy has taught me to be wholeheartedly present to whoever and whatever is before me in the moment. Right now, it's this book, but I can hear little feet making their way down the hallway, so in about ten seconds it will be Ralph. They sound like Ralphie's footsteps.

It was Ralph.

Being fully present is a beautiful gift to give someone.

Wholeheartedness was the first lesson. The key to living wholeheartedly is quite simple: just do one thing at a time. The second lesson is listening deeply.

I wasn't a very good listener before I discovered the speed of joy. It's not something you can excel at if you are doing something else at the same time. Listening is something you can only do well if you do it wholeheartedly.

Slowing down to the speed of joy taught me how to listen, really listen. I discovered that if you really listen, you can hear a person smile on the phone. I learned that people sound different when they're anxious, and silence can be a scream for help. I found out that children almost never talk about what they really want to talk about first. Not knowing if this is the right time, they talk about something else, to gauge your mood and to see if your body language reflects receptivity.

I learned to listen in new ways.

Laughter is a natural expression of joy. It's a wonderful indicator of well-being. People laugh when they're happy or when something is funny, but they also laugh to avoid a question, when they are nervous, or just out of relief.

When six people laugh at a joke, all six can be laughing for different reasons. The joke resonated with something from their past, but they are all drawing on different experiences. Listen closely and you will be able tell who didn't really think the joke was funny. That person's laugh will be forced, awkward, hollow, thin, less intense, shorter, and rather than trailing off naturally, will end abruptly—and their facial expressions won't surrender to the laugh.

When my daughter has had a tough day, she hugs me tighter. Sometimes it's what a person doesn't say that is the most important piece of the conversation.

Silence between two people can hold a myriad of messages and meanings.

You can tell who the saddest person in the room is if you set your heart to it—and you can find a way, however small, to comfort that person.

A sigh is a language unto itself. My wife has a hundred different sighs. A happy sigh, a sad sigh, a grateful sigh, a sigh that reveals excitement, a frustrated sigh, a "not this again" sigh, a hungry sigh, a hopeful sigh, a thoughtful sigh, an angry sigh, a curious sigh, a disappointed sigh, an exasperated sigh, a tired sigh, a "that was funny but I'm not going to laugh" sigh, a contented sigh, a romantic sigh, a "thank God this day is over" sigh, a sigh of acceptance, a joyful sigh, a "you remembered" sigh, a wistful sigh, and like us all, a sigh of relief. So many sighs.

The speed of joy is a wise teacher.

Three deeply personal lessons. The first was to be wholeheartedly present to the moment. The second was to listen deeply. And now the third.

Twenty years ago, when I wrote *The Dream Manager*, I wrote about our incredible ability to dream. Human beings can look into the future, imagine something *bigger and better*, and then, return to the present and work to make that richly imagined future a reality.

Everything great in history has been built by people who believed the future could be *bigger and better* than the past. That's what I used to believe.

I still believe that the three most extraordinary gifts God endowed us with are: life itself, free will, and our ability to dream.

I still believe our ability to dream is massively underemployed by most people.

I still believe we should use our God-given ability to dream to look into the future and envision new and exciting possibilities.

But I no longer believe that a better future *must* be bigger.

The *better* future God is calling me to is a *smaller* future. I'm confident of that.

A smaller future with less stuff and more connection with people. Less activity and more clarity. Fewer professional commitments and a chance to do my best work. A streamlined future with fewer email accounts, credit cards, apps, and subscriptions. A slower future and better relationships. Less busyness and more joy. Less distractions and more time to think. A more discerning future focused on the vital few. A smaller future and more peace of mind. Less later and more now.

The idea of a *smaller* future has filled my heart with hope again. I'm excited for my smaller future.

Bigger isn't always better, and small is beautiful. I know I am being called to a *smaller* future, and I think somebody, somewhere, needs to consider the possibility that our whole society would benefit from a *smaller* future.

Scale often leads us to be cruel and unjust to each other. Scale itself can be inhumane—cruel and indifferent to the suffering of others. Scale itself can be dehumanizing—humiliating, degrading, stripping away a person's dignity, making that person feel less than human.

How would the world be different if we structured it as if people really mattered?

Small is beautiful. Our perpetual quest for more and bigger needs to be tamed. I miss the small businesses in our communities. I love a great bakery, a quirky coffee shop, a charming stationary store, and of course, small bookstores owned and run by booklovers.

A *smaller* future might be a *better* future for everyone.

It was fierce mercy that led me to step off the merry-go-round of life a few years back, but even the fiercest mercy is a kindness.

When you are an author, the criticism that comes with sharing yourself with the world compels you to develop a resilience that protects you from malicious and thoughtless attacks. But it can also prevent good and necessary messages from getting through to you. Fierce mercy is intense. It refuses to be ignored. It demands that we confront difficult truths.

I needed some fierce mercy and I'm grateful for it today. Looking back now at the path I was on I can see everything that I would have missed out on if I had remained on that path. The sad thing is, I wouldn't have even known I was missing out.

So, if you need to take a new path or get off a merry-go-round in your own life, I want you to know that somewhere deep inside you have the courage to do it. It may be difficult. It may seem impossible. But just knowing what you need to do is a moment of grace. Take full advantage of it.

Slowing down to the speed of joy doesn't much suit my personality, but I am trying. Some days I rejoice in my progress. Some days I wallow in how foolishly I overcommitted myself again. I expect to have more of both days until I die. I'm just hoping the foolish days are fewer with each passing year.

# # #

I'm so excited for you. Your springtime is just beginning.

People often ask if it is possible to change. It is. The human spirit has an astounding capacity for change. I have witnessed it many times.

The most common question readers have asked over the past thirty years is: *Can people change?* But what we really want to know is, *Can I change?*

You can. You can change. You can remake yourself. You can rebuild your life. How? One choice at a time.

I know this answer may seem like an oversimplification, but I assure you it is the foundation of all change. Change is multifaceted and rarely does a single choice lead to the change we desire. But the compounding effect of small choices, made consistently over time, accumulate to create astonishing change.

For example, invest $1 each day for sixty-five years at a compounding rate of 9% and the result is over $1.4 million. It is more helpful and hopeful to focus on one choice at a time (save $1 a day) than to see change as a monumental task (save $1.4 million).

There is also something called a keystone decision, and we should always be on the lookout for these opportunities. A keystone decision is a single decision that is made today but has a compounding effect in your future. Habits are the perfect everyday example.

Taking your studies seriously in school is a keystone decision. Prioritizing your health is a keystone decision. Relocating to a new city or a different country is a keystone decision. The friendships you nurture are keystone decisions. Financial discipline is a keystone decision. Starting a business is another example. Deciding who to marry is one choice, but it is a keystone decision that sets in motion a ripple effect. H. Jackson Brown Jr. advises, "90% of your happiness or misery will come from who you decide to marry."

Deciding to take a break from traveling and speaking was the keystone decision that made the speed of joy possible for me. I didn't know it at the time, but it was. That single decision was equivalent to making a thousand small choices.

The point is: You can change. You can remake yourself and rebuild your life one choice at a time. Start making choices your future self will thank you for making.

Your mind will come up with lots of reasons why none of this is possible for you. That's just head trash. Head trash is the negative thoughts and limiting beliefs that clutter your mind and prevent you from striving for your full potential. These thoughts often escalate into fear, anxiety, self-doubt, and irrational assumptions that can prevent you from making progress or taking any action at all.

Head trash is mental clutter. Here are some specific examples: Fear of failure. Ruminating on past mistakes. Worrying about things outside your control. Believing you're not good enough. Fear of rejection. Brooding about perceived shortcomings. Obsessing over what other people think.

Any time you feel stuck, trapped, or in a rut, the obstacle is probably your own mental clutter (at least in part). Head trash is an obstacle to your new springtime. It's time to take out the head trash.

People say, "It's too late for me." It's a common example of head trash. I hear it from people in their fifties, people in their forties, and I hear it from thirty-somethings. A couple of weeks ago, I heard a twenty-one-year-old say it. Too late? All this reminds me of the first time I read Hugh Prather, and these words in particular:

> *"If I had only. . .*
> *forgotten future greatness*
> *and looked at the green things and the buildings*
> *and reached out to those around me*
> *and smelled the air*
> *and ignored the forms and self-styled obligations*
> *and heard the rain on the roof*
> *and put my arms around my wife*
> *. . . and it's not too late."*

I remember crying the first time I read these words. I didn't even know why I was crying, but I do remember being hungry, angry, lonely, and tired.

There was something about his longing that I shared. The whole reflection is about the things he wishes he had done but didn't, and then, the last line delivers all the hope and possibility we need to step boldly toward our future.

"*. . . and it's not too late.*"

Slow down.

Listen to the rain. Walk in the rain.

Put your arms around your husband, wife, boyfriend, girlfriend.

Breathe in the crisp morning air. Breathe deep. Feel the life within you.

Eat and drink, and taste, really taste. Savor.

Hug your sons and daughters. Hold them a little longer, and a little tighter. You never know when it will be the last time.

Speak your gratitude. Often. Blessed are those who feel appreciated, and those who make them feel appreciated.

Begin again. Today. Right now.

It's not too late.

Isn't it time, once and for all, finally and without reservation, to live a life that allows you to lay your head on your pillow at night knowing that who you are, and where you are, and what you are doing makes sense?

There is no good reason to spend the rest of your life suffering the joyless urgency that busy inflicts on us. . . and it's not too late.

I WISH YOU MANY

Each night before my children go to bed, I spend a few minutes with them, one at a time, talking about the day, reading, praying, asking questions and answering questions. It is a magical time in my day. It reorients me.

Children know the speed of joy. They have a way of effortlessly reminding us of what matters most. The clarity of a child can instantly rearrange our priorities. I had such an experience when my third son, Harry, was five years old.

"What are you going to do tomorrow?" I asked my five-year-old son. He thought for a moment, and then replied with pure delight, "I'm just going to wake up, have breakfast, and then I will decide."

It was one of those piercing moments of clarity that children effortlessly supply.

I smiled.

"That sounds amazing, Harry."

"Yep," he said, smiling back, "Tomorrow night I will tell you all about it," and off to bed he scampered joyfully.

But his words lingered.

Harry had figured it out and Hemingway's words came floating back, "When spring came, even the false spring, there were no problems except where to be happiest. . . and if you could keep from making engagements, each day had no limits."

Later that night I found myself reflecting on what my little boy had taught me. Days later, weeks later—his words were still resounding deep with me. They were an invitation to something more, better, different.

"When was the last time you woke up, had breakfast, and only then decided what to do that day?" I kept asking myself.

It had been a while. I couldn't think of one.

Since that night, I have endeavored to change that. I call them Harry Days. A Harry Day is a day when you wake up, have breakfast, and decide what will bring you the most joy.

I wish you many Harry Days.